Advanced Praise for *The Huma*

I0054231

As a student of Mary Pat Knight, I can say firsthand that *The Humanized Leader* belongs on the desk of all leaders. In this book she offers an engaging, practical roadmap to developing your emotional intelligence as a leader, so you can connect with, inspire, and guide the people you serve.

–Gino Wickman, Author of *Traction* and *Entrepreneurial Leap*

Mary Pat Knight's insights, guidance, and support helped us successfully navigate a major transformation in our company – a seismic shift that required me to step into a much higher level of leadership and service to our team. *The Humanized Leader* distills the best of her work into an easy-to-understand handbook that belongs on the desk of any professional who wants to elevate and honor the teams they lead.

–Marci Shimoff, NYTimes Best Selling Author of *Happy for No Reason* and *Chicken Soup for the Woman's Soul*

To successfully scale your business, you must evolve as a leader. The 'dictator' style of leadership no longer works. For your team to step up and take full ownership of their roles, you need to offer guidance, cheerleading, and support, while also creating space for your team to make mistakes and grow as individuals. Mary Pat Knight has cracked the code on how to bring your whole heart to your role as a leader and shares her formula for emotionally intelligent leadership in *The Humanized Leader*.

–Allison Maslan,
Wall Street Journal Best Selling Author of *Scale or Fail*

For over twenty years Mary Pat Knight has inspired my work in the world of transformational leadership. As a friend and a mentor, she's helped me uncover my strengths and skillfully given me the knowledge and the courage to be my most powerful and conscious self. In my speeches and classes, I am constantly quoting from Mary Pat who is not only a master teacher but is a woman who walks her talk. I'm beyond grateful that she's put her body of work into book form so that she can share her knowledge more extensively with those leading a planet that is crying for humanized leaders.

–Debra Poneman, Best-Selling Author and
Founder/CEO of *Yes to Success, Inc.*

The Humanized Leader is full of concepts and assignments that provide immediate value to any leader looking to improve their skills. The concepts are simple and yet extremely profound. Mary Pat's insight brings great clarity on how to become a better listener, navigate tricky conversations, and empower others with feedback. This is a must read for those who are ready to become a more effective leader.

–Kristie Clayton, COO/Integrator at BCR Wealth Strategies and
Founder/Visionary of The Female Integrator Mastermind

Elevating the genius within an organization begins with the people and the culture. Vital to creating agility, adaptability, and resilience is a culture rooted in Emotional Intelligence – with people always at the center. Mary Pat Knight skillfully coached our organization utilizing the principles outlined in *The Humanized Leader.*

–Nancy Wright, CEO Girl Scouts of Greater Chicago and
Northwest Indiana

In a literal sea of leadership books, *The Humanized Leader* stands out as an inspirational and practical roadmap for leaders to become the best version of themselves. At a time when authentic, trust-based leadership is needed more than ever, Mary Pat's volume is a quencher for the leader thirsty for the growth mindset of a modern leader.

–John Lucas, CEO Management Essentials

There is a change taking place in leadership that shows top-down, control-based leadership is on its way out. Heart-based leadership is on the rise and you need to be prepared to bring your full self to your job. This means connecting with your team by being courageous and caring in your communication. In *The Humanized Leader,* Mary Pat Knight does a brilliant job of demystifying what it really takes to embrace and embody whole-hearted leadership.

–Cathy Fitzhenry, Board Chairman Vistage Worldwide

The workplace of the future requires that you show up as your whole self. Employees crave authenticity – and they can sniff out ego-driven b.s. in a heartbeat. Mary Pat Knight has been a trusted guide to our organization. In this book, she offers the same honest, straight-shooting approach to transform into a whole-hearted leader. *The Humanized Leader* is ideal for anyone who wants to step into a high level of leadership – experienced and aspiring leaders alike.

–Steve Pearson, Chief Strategy Officer,
Principal – Contemporary Staffing Solution

Engaged leadership has never been more important in our workplaces, which have become increasingly complex. Leaders who show up with their whole hearts lift their teams, inspiring employees to bring their best, be their best, and do their best. If you're ready to play a role in this engagement transformation, Mary Pat Knight offers a practical roadmap for your personal and professional growth in *The Humanized Leader*.

–Karen Wilson, President/CEO MAKE Corporation

Peppered with thoughtful action assignments to help translate nice-to-know insights into easy-to-use strategies, *The Humanized Leader* is a guide for anyone who is serious about showing up as a more effective leader. Whether you want to become a better listener, navigate tricky conversations with ease, offer feedback that empowers rather than deflates, or free your team from the grip of endless drama, Mary Pat Knight offers the path to success. This book is a growth guide for the whole you as a leader, professionally and in your personal life.

–Susan Thaden, CEO CRi/From Now On

THE HUMANIZED LEADER

The Transformative Power of Emotionally Intelligent Leadership to Impact Culture, Team, and Business Results

MARY PAT KNIGHT

Ignite Press
Fresno, CA

Copyright © 2021, Mary Pat Knight

All rights reserved. No part of this book may be used or reproduced by any means, graphic, electronic, or mechanical (including any information storage retrieval system) without the express written permission from the author, except in the case of brief quotations for use in articles and reviews wherein appropriate attribution of the source is made.

Published in the United States by Ignite Press.
ignitepress.us

ISBN: 978-1-953655-20-2 (Amazon Print)
ISBN: 978-1-953655-21-9 (IngramSpark) PAPERBACK
ISBN: 978-1-953655-22-6 (Ebook)

For bulk purchase and for booking, contact:

Mary Pat Knight
Support@LeadersInspired.com

Because of the dynamic nature of the Internet, web addresses or links contained in this book may have been changed since publication and may no longer be valid. The content of this book and all expressed opinions are those of the author and do not reflect the publisher or the publishing team. The author is solely responsible for all content included herein.

Library of Congress Control Number: 2020922865

Cover design by Kathleen Cantwell
Edited by Reid Maruyama
Interior design by Jetlaunch Layout Services
Illustrations by Riley J. Knight

OTHER BOOKS BY MARY PAT KNIGHT

Humans at Work - an Anthology

*Dedicated to the greatest teachers of humanized leadership, my children.
Sam, Lia, and Riley, I could not love or respect or appreciate you more.*

ACKNOWLEDGEMENTS

If I could write an entire book acknowledging whom I am grateful for, it would give me great pleasure.

For now, I offer thanks and appreciation to soul sister, Cathy Fitzhenry, who always encourages and teaches me. Thank you to Susan Lindner who showed up one November and has been my writing partner and dear friend since.

Thank you to Everett O'Keefe and the team at Ignite Press for the wonderful hand-holding through the publishing process. A tip of the hat to Cathy Fyock whose writing retreat made the completion of this book possible.

Thanks to Sam Knight for the original editing of the manuscript. You made me a better writer! Thanks to Riley Knight for the illustrations that pepper the book. Thanks to Lia Knight for always contributing when technology creates roadblocks.

Most importantly, I acknowledge all the many teachers who have influenced my ability to become masterful as a leadership and emotional intelligence business coach – two Barbara's, one Sue, a Debra, a Jack, and a Bill W.

TABLE OF CONTENTS

Part 3: Performance Leadership

Part 4: Genius Leadership

INTRODUCTION

As is the case with most books, this has been an idea for quite some time. The final finishes, however, were completed during 2020. This year of complete upheaval made the need for humanized leadership all the more important.

Qualities such as kindness, direct communication, appreciation, and clear direction were needed and highly valued. That is still true today. As a humanized leader, you have a great privilege to serve while you lead. Role modeling the best of emotionally intelligent leadership, people will flock to you and want to be led by you.

This book, *The Humanized Leader*, provides a blueprint of the skills, abilities, and mindsets required to lead well into the remainder of this century.

You can read from start to finish as the concepts build upon the other. Or you can hop around to the topics that are hottest for you right now. You will do well if you read from your heart, as well as your head. Deceptively simple, the concepts and skills will help you transform into a better version of yourself. If you do the work that accompanies the reading, you will be different when finished.

Come join the movement at www.thehumanizedleader.com. We can change the world together!

1

THE BEST LEADERS BRING THEIR WHOLE SELVES TO THE TASK

We all stood there in complete shock and horror. It was unreal. The entire place was a burnt-out shell of a building. And there, in that instant, went our livelihood, our friendship, and our source of well-defined comfort. This is the beginning.

Over a period of several months, I knocked around and tried and failed and tried and failed to pick up another waitressing job. After all, the best actresses in town had to have their start in some restaurant somewhere! After accidentally dropping a full tray of ice teas onto the table of the men who owned the restaurant that took a chance on me, I could see that my options were becoming more limited.

Nothing kicked in and nothing seemed to grab me as an opportunity. I walked around in a shroud of victimhood, waiting for the next kick to come. And it did. In the form of a divorce. What?! I was too young to be married, let alone divorced.

It took some time, yet finally, my innate leadership took hold. I could be a rudderless victim, blaming others, taking no accountability, failing to communicate and offer feedback, unable to deal with conflict or take risks. Or...I could do the complete opposite and become the leader of my own life.

This is the journey. Wherever you are in your leadership journey, it is time to grab hold of the reins and become responsible for your leadership footprint.

For me, it took some time and I made a lot of mistakes. However, I had some wonderful people take chances on the promise they saw in me. I was mentored. I was forced to decide. I was held accountable. I was encouraged to learn and take risks. I was appreciated and I recovered from my mistakes. Along the way, I became a pretty good leader and had the privilege of developing hundreds of leaders in my journey.

What developed into a career of executive entrepreneurship was a deep belief in the humanity of leaders. When leaders dropped the positional posturing and chose authenticity and connection, incredible things happened. At minimum, fulfillment and satisfaction are possible, and at maximum, incredible business results and legacies.

For years I have been coaching my clients to bring their whole beings to both their business lives and personal lives. It's the compartmentalizing and shapeshifting from professional to personal that creates disconnection and callousness. My leaders were WHOLE LEADERS. Thus, Humanized Leadership was born. This book reflects the philosophies and skill sets necessary to become the Humanized Leader of your life and business.

Emotional intelligence (EQ) is at the core of humanized leadership. This is not a straight up book about emotional intelligence, although the skills that lead to this intelligence are paced out for you.

If you want to read about the theory and history and lists of EQ attributes, please pick up the wonderful books by Daniel Golemean, Travis Bradberry, or Justin Bariso.

Rather, this book is a pathway to the emotionally intelligent leadership that is central to the humanized leader. Step by step and skill by skill, you will come to understand what it takes to lead from deep within – the heart space. This is where compassion and empathy meet hardcore feedback and accountability measures.

There is nothing soft about emotional intelligence. The practice of knowing and managing emotions – yours and others' – is not intuitive and requires practice.

There is nothing soft about soft skills. It's some of the hardest and most confounding work you will do.

But I promise you it is all worth it. Relationships are richer, performance is better, and results are higher when you step into your emotionally intelligent leadership capabilities.

We are at a defining point in leadership thought and the humanized leadership of emotional intelligence is at the center of it. But emotional intelligence requires not only the understanding and management of emotions, but also communication leadership and performance leadership and learning to live more and more in your personal genius.

That's what this book offers you – a Four Part system to strengthen your effectiveness, satisfaction, and results.

What exactly is a Humanized Leader?

Remember this phrase – it is a powerful mantra – a humanized leader is FACTUAL, DIRECT, NEUTRAL, and KIND.

- FACTUAL: Humble enough to deal with facts, rather than opinions.
- DIRECT: Willing to speak, lead, and coach with a direct style so that everyone understands.
- NEUTRAL: Able to identify and manage triggers and emotions to maintain a neutral stance.
- KIND: Engaged in relationships in such a way that kindness rules.

A humanized leader is self-aware, knowing both their strengths and weaknesses and is willing to share both with their teams.

A humanized leader finds the level-set. Positional power is not the leading indicator; rather, collaboration, team, parity, and inclusion lead the way.

A humanized leader optimizes other humans – defining success, coaching for performance, offering feedback to improve, learning from all mistakes, and fertilizing the garden with abundant appreciation.

Ultimately, a humanized leader is just that – a human. A human who is willing to accept and appreciate the humanity in others.

The world needs your humanized leadership. This book is a call to action.

Are you willing to become the Humanized Leader in your own life?

The promise of *The Humanized Leader.*

The book offers an operating system that, if practiced, will upgrade all of your leadership skills and perspectives. The four parts of this system are:

1. **Emotional Leadership** - the awarenesses and skills that allow you to manage your emotional life and influence the emotional life of others.
2. **Communication Leadership** - the skills and practice that make you an impeccable listener, connector, collaborator, and concise communicator.
3. **Performance Leadership** - a path to create a culture of accountability through direction, course correction, agreements, and integrity building.
4. **Genius Leadership** - a means to blend personal core values with corporate core values, work on purpose, eliminate energy zappers, and develop your team.

Thousands of leaders have progressed through these four phases with astounding results. Personal relationships with spouses and children flourished. Families in business together found a balance between professional and family connection. Millions of dollars of revenue were generated as teams learned to row towards the same shore using shared leadership language and perspective. Careers flowered and big life changes were navigated.

Follow the plan.

PHASE I
EMOTIONAL LEADERSHIP

At the start is the concept of emotional leadership. This consists of the skills, abilities, mindsets, and heart sets that allow us to manage our own human emotions and support others to express theirs in a healthy way. You never would have seen a topic such as this in a leadership book from the 1970s or 1980s because we were told to "leave them (our emotions) at the door." As the leadership world has expanded, so too has the discovery that humans can't do that. The fragmentation of emotions – "Can I or can't I?" "Should I or shouldn't I?" – is not a part of our experience in modern leadership, especially as a humanized leader. We embrace the whole person in this wonderful world of ours – and that includes the behaviors, attitudes, and emotions that make us wonderfully human.

2

LEADERSHIP DEMANDS SELF-AWARENESS

Part One: The Gift of Self-Appraisal

Let's start at the very beginning. The foundational skill of leadership is self-awareness. Every little thing you do, every action you take, every word you speak, every emotion expressed or felt has a ripple effect. You are in the spotlight no matter what. People are inferring meaning from everything you do. People are judging, critiquing, applauding, or ignoring you. There is no rest for the leader.

The most important foundational skill that you can master is the skill of accurate self-appraisal. When you can analyze yourself, you will be propelled towards course-correction and improvement. When you know yourself and can see your strengths and weaknesses from a place of forgiveness and improvement, you will not only naturally improve, you will create an environment where others around you can improve as well.

Let's do that now.

This self-assessment is designed to provide you a baseline understanding of your strengths and weaknesses at this very moment. This assessment is adapted from live training conducted with hundreds of clients. It is a tool for self-analysis. Take this assessment now and then again at the conclusion of this book. It's amazing how much progress can happen in a short amount of time.

Go through the self-assessment questionnaire and, on a scale of 1 to 5, measure your *satisfaction* in the areas listed, with 5 being "extremely satisfied" and 1 being "totally unsatisfied." Be honest with yourself here. Add the numbers up for a baseline total. Take note of any rankings below 3 and any trends that emerge. If you rank a 5, note it as a strength. However, be sure not to overuse it. As you may know, leaning too heavily on your strengths can turn them into weaknesses over time.

The Humanized Leader Self-Assessment	Rate 1 (low) to 5 (high)
I regularly offer my truth in a frank, direct, neutral, and kind manner.	
I coach others to find their own solutions, avoiding the need to fix, have all the answers, or be right.	
I communicate decisions that may differ from popular opinion, without making others feel wrong.	
I listen deeply and understand facts and how to validate the speaker.	
I recognize that others have different communication styles and am able to adjust my own communication style to be relatable.	
I offer feedback in the spirit of improvement, focusing on facts and behavior rather than my opinion.	
I am willing to be vulnerable and role model authentic and transparent communication.	
I am clear in my performance expectations of others and allow others to know what success looks like.	
I regularly provide appreciation and recognition to my team.	
I take ownership of my challenges, avoid blaming others, and know my personal leadership is within my control.	
Total Number of Points (Up to 50 points maximum)	

With this assessment in hand, you have an idea of what your baseline is. The rest of this book will unfold by allowing you to take a deeper look at these areas where you are strongest and the ones where you need to improve. The book will also provide you with many suggestions and exercises for practicing. (If you would like a pdf of this assessment, please visit www.thehumanizedleader.com/Bonus)

You will hear this over and over again throughout the system: Emotional Intelligence and Leadership are able to be improved. It takes self-awareness and the willingness to practice a series of skills over time. You can create your own improvement!

Let's jump into the system.

Part Two: Understanding Leadership Modes/ Traditional versus Modern Leadership

Do you lead or manage? Neither answer is right or wrong. Do you lean more towards the comfort of managing or the familiarity of leading?

In terms of leadership/management, do you feel you are more traditional or more modern? Why?

But first, let's discuss what differentiates a traditional leader from a modern leader.

Barry is a traditional business leader. He believes the buck stops with him. He is responsible for the results and therefore must know all the details. He is meticulous about his inspection process and he takes his responsibilities very seriously. Do not challenge Barry because, in his position as leader, he is the one who knows the answers, understands the strategy, and is in communication with the level above him. He will communicate the goal and dictate the steps to achieve them. His motivations are supported by the company because they want results, too. Few people do much more than toe the line with Barry, perhaps other than gossip about him behind his back. They get the work done because they fear the consequences of not doing so.

Frank, at the other end of the spectrum, is a modern leader. He is very personable. He cares about your feelings, wants, and needs. He will go out of his way to make you feel that you are a valued part of the team. He is adept at sharing his vision for the project and for creating "esprit de corps" (or team morale). He listens to you, shares your concerns, and makes you feel important as a person. You may occasionally miss a deadline because you know it is okay, and the independence he offers you means you may sometimes go into a project with incomplete information. But, oh well, you are feeling good and the team is having fun together.

Which leader would you prefer? Neither and both would be a great answer.

Thousands of students later, here are the common traits of each type of leader.

The Traditional Leader	The Modern Leader
Micro-managing	Nurturing
Authoritative	Flexible
Requires Loyalty	Embodies an ownership mentality
Unilateral decision making	
Closed office door	Focused on improvement
Driven by the bottom line	Values communication
Supervisor/ Manager	Manages expectations
Command and control mentality	"Servant Leader" (puts the needs of the team and the values of the organization first)
Unapologetically direct	
Hierarchy and "chain of command"	Vision Leads by example
	Earns loyalty
Adheres to rules and procedures	Inclusive/collaborative decision making
Sets expectations	
Competitive	"Open door" policy
Thinks in terms of inferiority and superiority	Empathetic

The Traditional Leader	The Modern Leader
Does not involve employees in decision making	Relatable
Respected and feared	Values teamwork
Process-driven	Acts as a coach for their team
Goal-driven	Values workplace culture
Emphasizes structure	Feels they "work for the team"
Prescriptive	Values diversity
Rigid	Open-minded

One or both lists may provoke a strong emotional reaction. You will certainly have a preference as to which type of leader you want to be. Most lean towards the modern leader. Modern leadership is absolutely needed today. However, if you are ONLY a modern leader, you may be missing an entire portion of your job: the management portion where you are required to adhere to the processes, the to-do's, the goals in the strategic plan, the financial performance, and the legal/compliance issues that are necessary to run a business.

Modern leaders, in theory, are loved by their teams. But the activities that fall into the traditional category are necessary to keep the business going.

Can you see that components from both lists are needed for you to lead in a powerful, authentic, and effective way?

Traditional leadership (or management) is the job of running a business. You see the daily list, the monthly list, the annual list of things that move your business forward. You must manage people, projects, and processes. From a sole entrepreneur to a Fortune 500 company, there must be a management process, as well as systems of accountability, in place.

The modern leader is the part of you that inspires others, cares for them, engages with them, creates culture, fosters collaboration, encourages innovation, gets personal, and communicates in a heartfelt way. All of these attributes are very much needed in today's corporate environment.

The combination of these two styles creates a leader who leads from the heart, as well as the mind. This leader will understand the task at hand and clearly communicate expectations while also offering encouragement. This leader will encourage teamwork and collaboration while holding a firm line in achieving goals within agreed-upon timelines. This ideal leader will do what it takes to create an unbeatable culture but is also capable of making the hard decision to release employees who are not fit for that culture.

The traditional side of the leader will manage performance through process-based thinking and the modern side will manage performance through people.

To be an effective leader, you *must* be well-versed in both leadership styles and combine them effectively.

Personal Perspective

I remember conveying this concept to the Girl Scouts of Greater Chicago and Northwest Indiana. In this case, my clients were to become my teachers. Up until that point, all of my teams had been eager to describe their praise for the modern leadership style and found extreme fault with the traditional approach. This group had a different point of view. They collectively said, "I really prefer a lot of what can be found on the traditional side. That style of leadership creates security in meeting performance goals. It provides clarity about expectations and deadlines, as well as about consequences if we fail to achieve the necessary results. This creates good boundaries in which to perform our jobs and achieve results." They went on to add that the modern style of leadership creates emotional and psychological safety. From that day on, I have never taught this module without honoring the balance needed by drawing from both sides.

Your job is to have the self-awareness to understand in what areas you are overusing one and forsaking the other. Your best bet is to be the most authentic-to-you balance of a traditional and modern leader.

Leaders Throughout the Organization

Do you have to be manager, supervisor, or have a title in order to be a leader? The answer is a resounding "NO." A leader can bubble up from any part of any organization. Consider the hospitality industry. Walk into any hotel and you will notice an untitled (and likely lowly paid) housekeeper who is loyally followed by the rest of the team. Hopefully, this housekeeper is role modeling the best behavior. Through de facto personal leadership and team recognition of this fact, this person, without possessing a title, effectively leads the team. They have followers. Make that leader your friend!

I've got the title…now what?

What happens when someone is promoted into a "title" and not taught or coached in neither the modern leadership skills nor the technical skills required for traditional management? There is an internal struggle (of which they are likely unaware) between "positional power" and "personal power."

Positional Power

Have you ever been managed by an individual who was a leader in title but who did not have leadership qualities? Perhaps you were even this person. This is the manager who has a title and has not yet developed the necessary skills or attitudes to lead. Instead, they use positional power, the authority they derive from their title, to manage. The manager who has not been trained or encouraged to adopt leadership behaviors is a despot. They are a person who works through positional power. *"I have the title; you must do what I say."*

This manager is trouble waiting to happen. Sometimes feared and sometimes respected, they are never truly followed. When you top-down manage by relying on your title, your employees may never own their own power nor take full accountability for their own outcomes. Positional power kills engagement.

Personal Power

A leader works from the inside out with personal power. This leader moves people into action with influence, understands and manages emotions, offers empathy, and communicates effectively. They are clear about expectations and goals. They are curators of accountability. The result is that employees are led to their own outcomes, and there is a greater likelihood of reaching goals as a team.

Watch your best salesperson be promoted to sales manager without the necessary leadership skills or mindset. Watch the same thing happen when your best server gets promoted and is thrown into the role of restaurant supervisor. You have imbued positional power but failed to coach to personal power. Personal power arises from leadership qualities. Those qualities create influence and emotional management.

The manager tells and the leader influences. Those who are told are taught to be dependent and those who are influenced are taught to think for themselves from a place of purpose.

What Kind of Business Team Would You Like to Manage?

Let's recap.

For our purposes, let us recast the traditional leader as the "manager" and the modern leader as "leader."

The manager is focused on tasks while the leader is focused on people.

The manager emphasizes process and procedures while the leader emphasizes vision.

The manager offers direction and the leader offers inspiration.

The manager is a "doer" while the leader is focused on the quality of being.

Management is about performance and leadership is about presence.

As always, you have a choice in every moment. Which part of your tool kit will you bring to every situation?

Part Three: Creating a Strategic Leadership Action Plan

You dream of becoming a stronger, better, more stable leader. You dream of being able to inspire the team with your vision. You dream of creating a culture of problem solvers, of accountability.

"A goal without a plan is just a wish."

– Antoine de Saint-Exupéry

Your dream must be articulated as a goal or an outcome that you desire. The first task of leadership is to translate that dream into a specific plan of action.

Closing

This chapter began and ended with exercises in accurate self-appraisal. It is vital to be self-aware. This is different from being self-centered. Your awareness of self includes the impact you have on others and on real-life situations. There is no "right" or "wrong" in self-appraisal, and no defensiveness is necessary. You are simply aware of the impact these qualities can have on yourself and others and can make choices that arise from self-awareness.

These choices should be derived from a proper mixture of traditional and modern leadership styles. Remember: a blend of the two is like a tasty stew.

Finally, with this analysis in hand, you are prepared to set goals and determine your desired outcomes. You can stop dreaming about what could be and begin translating your desire into a plan that can be measured with tangible results.

As you progress through this book, come back to this part of Chapter Two often. You will continue to add new goals and outcomes. When you plan this way, victory comes swiftly.

Stay inspired!

Action Steps

Before delving further into the concepts offered in this book, take an hour or so to complete your personal plan. Plan to revisit and update it as you progress through your reading. Use the following steps:

1. Take stock of the current state of your leadership. Complete your personal SWOT analysis. SWOT stands for Strengths, Weaknesses, Opportunities, or Threats. Opportunities and threats can come later in your process, especially if you are leading a business. For now, make a list of your strengths and your weaknesses.

2. Review your list and rank your results in order of importance or leverage. From the weakness perspective, what is causing the most distraction that, if addressed, would free up space for better leadership choices. From the strengths perspective, what is the highest priority focus that, if addressed, is the one action that will eliminate three or four other issues when improved or leveraged?

3. Pick one (for now). State your outcome with an expiration date in order to keep you on track and to provide a tool for future measurement.

4. Create a SMART action plan to make incremental improvements. This action plan determines milestones and to-do's that must be completed in order to achieve your desired outcome. SMART stands for Specific, Measurable, Actionable, Realistic, and Time-bound.

5. Shift into action and acknowledge the accomplishments that bring you closer to your desired outcome with each step.

3

EMOTIONAL LEADERSHIP - MINDSET AND HEARTSET

The Leadership Mindset

The human brain is a wonder to behold. When it is married with spirit and intention, there is little to stop what can be created. If you want to become the leader you envisioned in Chapter Two, you must address and manage your mindset.

What would you prefer? "I can't" or "I am able"? "I don't know" or "I'm confident that I can find out how"? Feelings of inability come from a place of doubt. You have plenty of evidence to make the second phrase option true.

It's estimated that there are about 100 billion neurons in the brain with maybe 100 trillion neural connections to boot. You've got a big brain.

The problem? You have two different agendas operating. You have your conscious brain, which is only the tip of the iceberg in terms of neurons and synapses, and your subconscious brain, the remainder, which is hidden from sight. We don't need to pit one against the other. What is important is to understand that most of our agendas are running in our subconscious but can be sent forward into the conscious. Both sides are always working together.

By combining your intentionality (free will and decision making) with your frontal lobe's functions (creativity/connections/outcomes), you can pull forth from the subconscious whatever evidence you need from experience, connecting meanings, and learning to enhance your self-confidence.

This beautiful relationship between your willpower and your creative frontal lobe allows you to make decisions, see connections (between ideas or memories) that others cannot, and foster innovation. As a leader, you must practice calling forth "evidence" from the subconscious.

Napoleon Hill talks of this in his seminal book, *Think and Grow Rich,* as he describes how the subconscious mind translates the thoughts you hold in your head into their physical equivalent. He identified this as the Law of Autosuggestion. "Like the wind which carries one ship East and another West, the Law of Autosuggestion will lift you up or pull you down, according to the way you set your sails of THOUGHT."

Michael Bernoff, author of *Average Sucks,* teaches about the subconscious file manager who is always sifting and sorting through the subconscious. Without direction, the file manager is likely to bring forward all kinds of errant memory files. Your job is to be conscious and deliberate about what you want to become conscious of. Why not give yourself an edge by deliberately and frequently bringing forth those memories that build self-confidence?

Managing Emotional State

Ask yourself: what have you been told about emotions, expression of emotions, and – especially – emotions in the workplace? What has this made you come to believe about these subjects? If you are like most people, you may have been led to believe that emotions don't belong in the workplace. Suck it up and save it for home! The immortal and incredulous words of Tom Hanks in *A League of Their Own* will forever sum up this paradigm: "There is no crying in baseball."

Let's get current. Emotions belong in the workplace, no matter what you have been told or have believed up until this point. Emotions are natural and even the most stoic people aren't unemotional. When it's said that emotions belong in the workplace, however, it does not mean emotions need to be brought into the workplace needlessly. Rather, it's an admission that emotions are natural and, by right, a part of the human experience.

Who works for your company? People do. Your company's employees are human beings that have been hired to deliver some kind of result. The common trait that all humans share is that we are complex, emotional beings. We would be foolish to deny this.

Imagine that you are holding a beach ball. The beach ball represents whatever emotion you are experiencing. You are in a swimming pool of all your experiences, responsibilities, and relationships, holding onto this ball of emotions that you feel you cannot, or should not, express.

You shove the beach ball under the water as deep as possible. Pushing down hard, you feel the resistance building until, unable to bear the pressure, the ball splashes to the top and sprays everyone in sight. Just like the beach ball, you cannot push down your emotions for long before they surge back to the surface in one way or another.

A proactive leader will find a way to responsibly recognize and manage their own emotions and those of their team members.

That's where Emotional Intelligence comes into play.

Emotional Intelligence

What is EQ? In its simplest form, Emotional Intelligence boils down to understanding yourself, knowing you have emotions and managing the emotions you are feeling. At the same time, having emotional intelligence requires understanding that other people have emotions, too, and that we manage the relationships that are created out of that understanding.

While emotional intelligence falls under the umbrella of "soft skills," or interpersonal skills, don't think it is easy to acquire. These so-called "soft skills" are high-level leadership skills. To master emotions, to develop relationships, to deal with humanity – these are some of the hardest skills to acquire, practice, and master.

Several workplace studies, including one conducted by LinkedIn, "*LinkedIn Learning 2020 Workplace Learning,*" have identified emotional intelligence as one of the most powerful sets of skills and abilities you can master for the next few decades. It shifts the focus away from IQ, a measure of one's reasoning ability compared to the general population as determined by a problem-solving test. Before the 1990's, IQ and reasoning ability were considered the ultimate hallmarks of overall intelligence. EQ, as opposed to IQ, is a measure of interpersonal and communication skills. It's the "heart" – the self-knowledge, interpersonal awareness, and emotional management – which balances and completes the "head" of reasoning and problem solving.

Maybe you are one of those who have been taught that feelings don't belong in the workplace and should be left at the door. You may find yourself left behind as workplaces become more holistic, balancing work and life. The strict work/domestic boundaries of the past no longer hold. You are a human being and human beings feel – no matter where you are. The leader's job is to embrace emotionality without getting lost in feelings. This will allow you to leverage the full potential of all your employees and of yourself. Everybody wins.

Emotional Intelligence may fly in the face of traditional management theory where the boss is the boss and the workers work. EQ demands a rewiring of much of what you believe about "command and control" leadership. It requires that you clean your personal filters of outdated beliefs, habits, and paradigms and experience personal transformation. Your businesses, lives, and world expects this and needs this now. Are you ready?

The EQ Matrix

Let's look at the basic premise of EQ. This matrix was inspired by the work of Daniel Goleman, a pioneer in the EQ movement. The left side of the matrix is about you. You have emotions (top left quadrant) and, to be effective, you must manage those emotions through self-management techniques (bottom right quadrant). On the right side, those with high emotional intelligence also recognize that other people have emotions (top right quadrant) and because of that, have some great strategies for managing relationships or interpersonal environments (bottom right quadrant).

Human beings are tricky. What ought to be clear-cut and based on common sense can become murky and complicated.

Have you ever looked back and realized that you had spent an inordinate amount of energy justifying an emotion (usually negative)? Think of the last time someone hurt you or disappointed you. How much time did you spend finger-pointing and blaming? Self-control goes out the window and responsiveness becomes reaction, optimism morphs into resistance. In such a frame of mind, how could you possibly even try to understand where the other person is coming from, much less elevate the environment or promote collaboration?

On the other side, recall a time when you were more than a little mixed up in nursing the feelings of another person. Compassion can turn into empathy, which too often turns into emotional enabling. There is no managing the relationship or the environment because you have taken your eyes off the bigger picture to fixate on one person's suffering.

Emotional intelligence asks us to take a step back with some deep breaths and understand that everyone is wired to have emotions. Emotions may pop up from anywhere, from any stimulus, from any trigger. The skill we are building is to see them, to get to a neutral set point and make some choices about how we want to respond. This takes practice and a gradual unwinding of old patterns and mindsets.

Choice and Compassion

There are two more components to our model which flesh out your job as a leader with EQ and supporting the EQ in others: compassion and choice.

On the horizontal axis, imagine the word "choice" in between the top and bottom boxes. In the moment you recognize an emotion, you have a choice. This choice determines if you are going to manage how you express your emotion or if you are going to react without thought or consciousness.

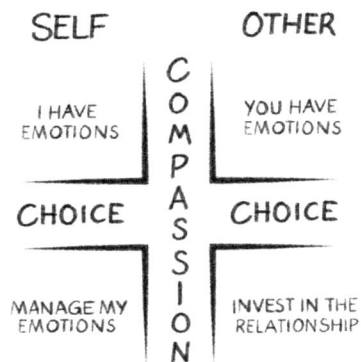

SELF	COMPASSION	OTHER
I HAVE EMOTIONS		YOU HAVE EMOTIONS
CHOICE		CHOICE
MANAGE MY EMOTIONS		INVEST IN THE RELATIONSHIP

Imagine you are feeling the emotion of anger. If you are unconscious of your emotional state, you may be led to yell or point fingers or criticize or shut others down. If you remain aware of what you're feeling, you will identify your emotion and choose how to express it. That's the choice point. You must first recognize the emotion and then prompt yourself to choose how you deal with it. Rather than yelling, maybe you say, "I'm feeling angry right now. It's not your fault, I'm just feeling angry." Or maybe you choose to take a 5-minute mental break so that you can return to a powerful neutral place.

The power of choice is amazing.

Examining the same example on the other side of the matrix, you see someone on your team is angry. You can choose to judge or deny or prohibit the emotion, provoking an even worse outburst or emotional shutdown. Or you can choose to reflect the emotion, gently bringing attention to it and supporting the other to find a healthy way to express or deal with it.

That's managing the relationship!

On the vertical axis rests a magnificent word, "compassion." Empathy is a high-level leadership EQ skill and compassion is empathy on steroids. Empathy permits you to recognize and understand why another person may be experiencing whatever emotions they are currently feeling. Compassion is a wise place of holding space. You may never understand why the other person is feeling or expressing the emotion they are, yet you can hold a space for them to feel it and figure it out for themselves. It's a place of non-judgement. It creates incredible emotional safety.

Compassion allows us to forgive ourselves for poor expressions of our emotions and permits us to observe, assess, and ultimately coach others as they are expressing their own emotions.

Choice and compassion are powerful leadership companions to understanding and supporting ourselves and others in the EQ matrix. To practice and demonstrate both qualities is a rare and valuable combination in the workplace.

EQ is the mindset miracle, leading to joy and satisfaction in our relationships and with yourself.

How Do I Improve as an Emotionally Intelligent Leader?

Emotional intelligence can be developed. EQ is a set of skills, abilities, beliefs, paradigms of thinking, and behaviors that can be developed and changed over time. It's not about personality. It's about action and performance. And it's not about behavioral traits. Rather, it's about core attributes and conscious self-management of thoughts and emotions.

The only way to improve EQ readiness is to practice. Be prepared to make some mistakes and use those mistakes as learning opportunities. Your mastery of emotional intelligence will make you a unique and valued leader, creating emotional safety for those around you. Emotional safety promotes the desire to risk, be bold, be honest, and achieve outstanding results.

There is a Payoff to the Team

What do you think about the impact of developing your emotional intelligence on the development of your team?

Many studies – using various EQ modules – show that there is a powerful contribution to overall team performance when the leader is more emotionally intelligent. Higher-performing employees tend to increase the overall organization's productivity. There is a real benefit to developing these qualities and skills.

A study conducted by Talent Smart tested emotional intelligence, alongside 33 other important workplace skills, and found that emotional intelligence is the strongest predictor of performance, highlighting a full 58 percent of success in all types of jobs. In that same study, 90% of top performers have a higher emotional quotient and make $29,000 more annually than their lower EQ counterparts.

There are many additional studies that prove that EQ adds an element of trust, connection, and communication that elevates personal and team performance.

To Sum It Up

EQ is about understanding the emotions that you experience and that you see in others. Understanding the human experience of emotions allows you to regulate your expression and support others to that end, as well. The outcome is productive relationships.

When self-awareness elevates, you can better choose how to express your emotions. Furthermore, you have enhanced self-confidence which permits you to take targeted action.

And what you see and understand in others can create a safe space for them to recognize their own emotions and make better choices. What does that look like?

- Relationships are managed through awareness and high regard for others.
- You are self-aware and practice self-acceptance, the ability to be aware of and accept oneself.
- You are aware of the feelings, concerns, and needs of others.
- Emotional expressions are managed and self-owned and others are not blamed.

The payoff? You have the ability to be realistic and put things in the correct perspective. When you can be realistic and neutral and have the correct perspective, there is no room for drama. You and others are drawn to a positive disposition and outlook on life. When a team believes it can win, it does. When a team believes it can produce, it does.

If you'd like to find out more about how you stack up in your emotional intelligence, you can take a quick quiz here: www.emotionallysmartleader.com

Triggers

No matter how much structure and support we put into place, it is inevitable that at some point we will be emotionally triggered. It usually happens in the most unexpected ways and at the most inconvenient times and places. But it happens.

An emotional trigger is any topic that makes us feel uncomfortable (or return us to the feelings of an initial trauma). These emotional triggers are telling us which aspects of our life we might feel frustrated or unsatisfied with. It can vary in each person because we are all struggling with something different.

"It's the little moments that trigger some of our most outsized and unproductive responses."

– Marshall Goldsmith, *Triggers: Creating Behavior That Lasts*

The swiftness of a trigger point can often leave us reeling and out of our leadership mindframe, propelling us into reactive behavior and feelings of woundedness.

We began this chapter with emotional intelligence because we must first become attuned to our emotions as we are experiencing them and learn how to manage our responses to them before addressing emotional triggers. That way when a rogue trigger presents itself, the cards are already stacked in our favor.

Remember the horizontal axis of choice found in the EQ matrix. Just prior to the choice point is where you will find the trigger. Something has happened, you saw something, you heard something, and as a result you were unconsciously transported back in time to the first incidence of discomfort. You aren't even aware that this is happening. It's as though your brain and your emotions are hijacked. You experience a big, destabilizing emotion.

Good news! If you have been building your EQ muscles, you will recognize the emotion and remember that you have a choice in how you manage and ultimately express it. If it grabs you by the throat and hijacks your self-management abilities, all bets are off, and you are off to the emotional racetrack on a horse stung by a bee.

How do you know you are about to experience an emotional trigger? The good news is that there are always clues. Much like a poker tell (which is the little tic or eye movement or sigh that sends a foretelling signal to the other players) that allows you to dominate someone in the game of poker, you have a trigger tell, which gives you the advantage once you are aware of it. Some people feel their pulse quicken. Others feel their skin flush. Some report head buzzing or chest pounding. Still others become short of breath or begin to sweat. What's common about these clues? That's right: they are all physical reactions to emotional stimuli.

When you feel any of these physical clues, you can rest assured that you are being given an invitation into an emotional trigger. Accept the invitation at your own peril.

A shrewd emotional leader will follow the EQ instructions and acknowledge the feeling, knowing it is likely to pass, and pause to employ a de-escalation strategy before deciding how to respond.

What are some of your favorite de-escalation strategies? Listed below are several suggestions by students of the Leadership Mastery™ program over the course of several years:

1. Take three deep breaths
2. Pause for 90 seconds while breathing
3. Take a time out
4. Physical activity – like walking or jumping jacks
5. Admit that you are triggered and ask for a moment to collect your thoughts
6. Table the discussion until tomorrow
7. Ask yourself, "What am I really feeling here and why?" and then make a choice to let it go to the best of your ability

Once the initial 90 second physical response has passed, you have a choice to make – much like the choice of emotional response in the EQ matrix. Do you want to hold onto and nurse the feelings that don't serve you? Or can you recognize the trigger, release the feelings, and move on with your best leadership self?

The Consequences of not Managing your Emotions

What is the impact on team and team trust when the leader is triggered? This is a story that one of my mentees and facilitators brought to one of his groups and it has merit as an illustration of how a trigger point can affect not only you, but also your employees.

Imagine yourself as George, the general manager – the operating leader – of a decent-sized hotel. The entire pace and execution of the operation emanates from your leadership. As a good leader, you know each of your employees by name and frequently walk through the hotel to inspect and engage.

It's a busy day. You have just received a call from your regional manager that not only must your budget be scrubbed and re-submitted, but that the brand inspectors will be at your property in a few hours for the dreaded brand inspection. Stress is mounting, yet you have it all together. Until...

On the 5th floor of the hotel, as you are conducting room inspections, Maria (a long-tenured housekeeping employee) confronts you in the hallway.

"Mr. George, you are coming to look at my rooms. But they are not ready. Lewis came and took my vacuum and without my vacuum I can't complete my rooms. I need my vacuum back."

Your last nerve has finally been plucked. You go emotion-blind and become triggered by the request for resources from your staff (or is it the new budget or the inspection or...) and you snap.

"Maria, the vacuum is NOT yours. All the vacuums belong to the hotel...Not to YOU. You do not get a special vacuum. There is no Maria vacuum. Now go on back and finish up your room and I will find one of the HOTEL vacuums to bring to you to finish your work!!!"

Oh my. Congratulations. You have trotted off to the land of drama. One wrong turn and there you are. What happens next is gossip. Maria tells her cousin, also a housekeeping employee, who then tells Jim. At the lunch break Jim and Maria are commiserating over what a mean boss George has become. Five people overhear and join the conversation. The next day, the rest of the housekeeping staff joined the "Mr. George is a meanie" campaign.

How long does it take George to win back the trust and engagement of his housekeeping staff? Krispy Kreme doughnuts will not patch this one up. It may take months, a year, or maybe never – despite being on best leadership behavior from there on – to patch it up.

The stakes are high, my friends. You need to give yourself an advantage by:

1. Practicing understanding the emotions you are feeling
2. Practicing choosing productive behaviors from emotion identification
3. Accepting the fact that you are going to be triggered from time to time
4. Learning to recognize your own physical clues
5. Employing a de-escalating strategy to move you back into leadership

What Happens When Someone on the Team is Triggered

A habit that Stephen Covey shares in his seminal text, *The 7 Habits of Highly Effective People,* is to sharpen the saw, which means to practice and practice until you are able to do the activity with little forethought. He suggests that one of the best ways to do this is to teach what we have learned.

By reminding yourself of the right-hand side of the EQ matrix while avoiding judging or criticizing the emotions of others, you support them to understand and express what they are feeling in a constructive way. Always with an eye on the relationship, you teach them about triggers and help them find a great way to realize when they are triggered, as well as strategies to de-escalate. If they have expressed their triggered emotion in a poor way, as George in our story did, you will offer them feedback and coaching to improve. The good news is that the rest of this book will offer you key skills and perspectives to have a leadership influence on your entire team.

Support for the Leader - You May Need A Lifeline, not a Pity Party

Do you remember the game show *Who Wants to Be a Millionaire?* It was exciting, surprising, and nerve-wracking to witness who would roll the dice, what they knew, and when they needed help. A key tool was the "lifeline." When stuck, the player could cast a lifeline to someone in their life who they felt could offer the best support in that situation.

Who Is Your Leadership Lifeline?

This is a special kind of friend or colleague who will not argue for your limitations. Rather, they will call you to a higher place of wisdom and action. They will not let you sit in your own stew for long. Instead, they will help you find your contribution and your creative way to solve your issue. They will not rescue you or pity you. What they will do is compassionately hold space or wisely ask the right questions to get you moving again.

You are going to get triggered by a person, place, or thing *(think your politically opposite relative at the last family gathering)*. Human nature says to sit in the trigger, justify the feelings, judge others, and be righteous in our own misguided feelings. When not making conscious emotional decisions, you will seek out those friends and colleagues who will agree with you, help you justify your position, pat your head, sit in judgement with you, and help you stay stuck in your righteousness. Let's be real… *we've all either done this or been that person.*

The person who acts as your lifeline won't play the justification game with you. That's why they may only be the third or fourth person you reach out to. You reach out to them when you are tired of emotional yes-men. You see the wormhole you are about to descend into and need that extra boost to stay the leadership course. Thank heaven for lifeline friends!

This is what you look for in support and what you can do to be a lifeline support to your team:

- **Be neutral** and don't take on the other person's issue or point of view
- **Stay open** to their experience without judgment of the feelings they are having
- **Hold an intention** that they are greater and more powerful than the trigger they are currently experiencing. You hold that intention strongly
- **Ask great open-ended questions** that help them to make leadership decisions.

- **Offer wisdom or feedback directly** when appropriate and without leading them with your own agenda
- **Don't take credit for the outcome,** remembering you are a vehicle – a lifeline – for them to create their own powerful outcomes

When you accept your own feelings and triggers and learn to manage them well, you become a beacon of hope for others who are still navigating these tricky waters. The other skills you will learn in the subsequent chapters of this book including listening, inquiry, feedback, and coaching will set the stage for you to be a *JEDI-MASTER Trigger Lifeline.*

Final Thoughts About Managing Workplace Emotions

Reminder: the only emotions that you can manage and control are your own. You can influence the emotions or expressions of emotion (behavior) of another by your example, your compassion, and your leadership. Paying attention, validating, and coaching are your key tools to managing the relationship at all times – and most importantly when high emotions are at stake.

Action Steps

Do a little self-reflection right now. Pull out your journal or some journal pages. For the following questions rank yourself from 1-10 and write down your first thoughts on how to improve and be more effective. This will set a solid baseline.

1. How well do you know yourself?
2. How well do you manage stress and curveballs?
3. How easily do you understand what you are feeling?
4. How well do you express what you're feeling?

5. How well can you solve problems and make decisions in the face of emotions?
6. How well do you create and maintain relationships?
7. How accurately can you assess a situation in the moment, stepping back, and assessing what is happening while seeing all sides, then choosing the correct action or response intuitively?

What are you willing to take action on? Hold onto this assessment. You will be pleased that by the end of our time together, there will be marked improvement.

4

YOU'VE GOT TO TAKE A RISK - GETTING OUT OF THE COMFORT ZONE

Comfort Zone

A key leadership job is to take intelligent risks while assessing where limiting beliefs, old habits, and overused behaviors have you stuck.

Intelligent risks balance strategy with self-awareness.

Imagine a bubble. The comfort zone is a nice bubble of protection, a good barrier to keep you safe from the outside world. You rest on familiar furniture, surrounded by the books you like to read and the TV shows you like to watch.

You know how to do things competently with relatively little stress. You know which rules to bend and those you must keep. You are confident that what you think and believe is true. You feel successful and secure. You don't have to second-guess or question your choices or behavior.

Along with your thoughts and patterns and beliefs, you will find familiar people. Your family, your pets, your spouse, your partner, your kids, your neighborhood, the people from the school that you went to are all around you. You are safe.

Is it wrong to be there? No, not at all. Is it self-limiting to stay there? Yes, if you want to grow as a leader and as an emotionally intelligent human being. Staying in your comfort zone too long creates stagnation and procrastination and sometimes depression.

What happens when you stay in your bubble too long? You find yourself moving closer and closer to the edge, but not leaping into that unknown area outside of the sphere. You may feel frustrated or stifled. Your world starts to feel small. You may find yourself becoming angry with the people who were enjoying this space with you. You get to the boundary of the sphere and the itch to leap gets stronger and stronger.

Think back on a time when you wanted to take a big risk – to go to college, get married, start your business, or take on a more important role in a company for which you didn't feel ready. You bumped up against the edge of safety, the boundary of your comfort zone. It's natural to question yourself during these times. Taking that risk means you have to change and be different. You have to do new and unfamiliar things which takes you to an unknown place. You are no longer safe.

The protection of the comfort zone is palpable and, faced with a perceived lack of safety that comes with a big risk, many people choose to remain inside the comfort zone, not moving or growing until they need to. Until it becomes painful.

"Don't live the same life every year for 75 years. That's no life."
- Anonymous

When you are ready, and not quite there, here is what you are likely to experience: You feel nervous. With sweaty hands or butterflies in your stomach, you don't know if what you're feeling is fear or excitement. You question things and experience doubt. Soon you begin to hear the voices of the "itty bitty shitty committee" (yes, it's real and, yes, I did just write "shitty") saying, "You are too old. You don't have enough education. Stay safe. Don't go. Stay here with us. You know what you know here.

You don't know what you don't know out there. We don't do it that way in our family."

Anxiety and uncertainty collide with your desire to jump. And those awful voices keep getting louder with their admonitions urging you to stay put. You feel that it's probably better just to stay where you are. It's not.

Somewhere outside the comfort zone is a risk worth taking. It's a North Star for you. That star is blinking at you, tempting you with that thing you want or that person you desire to become. Maybe you want to pursue a master's degree or purchase a new house or commit to a relationship. It's there; it's blinking at you. You are tormented by the "should I or shouldn't I?" internal debate. You stand at the precipice and your anxiety turns into a feeling of fear, of uncertainty coupled with thoughts that urge you to stay put. Again, you are tempted to just stay where you are.

Don't.

When that worthy goal or outcome just out of your comfort zone calls to you, find a way to leap. Even taking one tiny step towards it creates momentum and expansion.

Leap.

You did it! How do you feel? Do you feel proud? Maybe a little scared and nervous as well? You got to the edge of the comfort zone and experienced all the feelings and negative voices that come with it, and still you stepped forward. Your expansion creates a higher level of self-confidence and self-assuredness.

With your step, you have created a bigger comfort zone. You know what that means! With the next step forward, you will face yet another barrier of self-doubt, fear, and the voices once again. However, you have proven to yourself that forward movement is possible because you did it once before. Even though the next step causes discomfort, you have rewired your brain from the reptilian position of fight, flight, or freeze to the leadership brain of expansion. Expansion becomes desirable and you are willing to suffer a little discomfort to have it. Every time you take a risk, your horizons expand.

Let's expand a little on the word "risk." Risk doesn't mean you always achieve your desired outcome. It's a bonus when you do. Risk means that you're willing to try something different, you're willing to question a thought, you're willing to challenge a belief, and you're willing to expand beyond where you currently are. Rarely undramatic, it often happens in baby steps.

Perhaps the distance from the center of your comfort zone to the worthy goal that is calling to you is too far. Why don't you do it in five or six steps? Those represent five or six additional risks and each opportunity to take a risk creates more opportunity to stretch, strengthen, and grow. Many humans are risk-averse, and an incremental step approach to growth is a great way to progress and gain confidence over time.

As a human being, you are faced with choices every day. You have a basic choice to stay put (stasis) or to take a few chances (expansion). Humans have been put on this earth to grow and learn – that's expansion.

When you're inside the zone, you may simply be satisfied and feel safe and choose to stay where you are. Often, though, you find yourself observing those who are expanding outside of theirs, and you may find yourself protecting your personality and your choices. This can show up as denial, bad habits, and comparison. You might feel defensive or you might take a righteous stand for your position. You may judge and criticize the choice of others who are different from you. These are all protected behaviors and we have all experienced them. Welcome to humanity.

When you choose to expand outside of your zone, you will have a different kind of experience. You are taking risks which produce excitement and adrenaline. You are curious and willing to explore. You are learning new things, which produces additional questions and connections. Self-confidence grows and you are more optimistic about what comes next. You make mistakes and the expansion calls upon you to learn from the mistakes and grow even more.

Is it ever OK to go back to the comfort zone?

Of course. Remember the old TV show, *Cheers*, where everybody knows your name? Sometimes you are tired of stretching and growing or you've hit a bump and just need to go someplace familiar where, to continue the Cheers theme song, "They are always glad you came." Refresh and renew, gather your strength and then out you go again.

Personal Perspective

You know you can get a little too comfortable and outstay your welcome. I think of my youngest, Riley, who remains to this day a great teacher to me. He chose a university more than 800 miles away. Jumping out of his comfort zone, he lived on his own, managed his schedule, made his own choices without parental oversight. He played, he studied, he passed! He came home for the summer and found himself right smack dab in the middle of an old yet familiar zone – living in Mom's house. He rested, played, relaxed for a period. Soon, he found himself regressing back to his 16-year old self, complete with undisciplined habits and old ways of thinking. He became restless and unhappy. Staying a little too long in a former comfort zone, it had become too small for him. Familiar, temporarily re-energizing, but ultimately it did not fit him anymore.

Lesson learned. Once you've moved out of the family home, it is very difficult to move back home. You've changed. You've expanded. You are different. That zone doesn't fit any more. Apply this lesson to any area of your life that you have been tempted to return to. Once you jump out of an original comfort zone, you CAN return…but only shortly. Get recharged and then get the heck out of there!

The Comfort Zone and Change Management

Those of you who are responsible for managing change in your businesses will face big challenges when you rub up against other people's comfort zones. Unless you clearly articulate steps, benefits, and the long-term vision, you will be met with resistance and fear. Make it safe for people to change by clearly and regularly communicating and painting the full picture of the step-by-steps and then taking hold of a few hands who can lead the way.

Change asks us to take a different view of the world. Change brings chaos. Chaos brings innovation and creativity.

Think about a recent major change – either work or personal – in your life:

- What were your initial reactions or feelings?
- How do you feel about it right now?
- Was one of your initial responses fear – in some form or another?

This relates directly to the comfort zone conversation. Many fears change to some extent. Familiar with your situation, you are comfortable whether the situation is productive or not.

There are four distinct phases people experience when invited out of the comfort zone and into the change process:

1. Shock: Squarely and firmly in the center of the comfort zone
   - It will never work
   - Disbelief
   - Unwillingness to risk
2. Defense: Squarely and firmly in the center of the comfort zone
   - Unyielding
   - Angry, negative
   - Fear
   - Dig heels in
3. Acknowledge: Still in the comfort zone yet readying to leap
   - Sadness and a feeling of loss
   - Gradual recovery of confidence
   - Problems brought out into open
4. Adaptation: Leap from comfort zone into expansion
   - Enthusiasm, excitement, and commitment replace distrust and fear

When new processes are confusing, the move to adaptation is bumpy. Encourage your team to ask questions and clarify information, knowing there are no silly questions. For you, practice patience, answer every question, champion, and cheerlead; if you don't know the answer to a particular concern, then find out.

Become a Change Agent

When coaxing another from their comfort zone, a place where they feel safe and smart, you will need to become a change agent. That involves helping people to adapt to the new reality and understanding some of their underlying emotions, thoughts, and beliefs. It's important to note that with proper execution through a path of change (listed below), your biggest skeptics may convert to your most vocal champions. Your job is to make the change actionable and palatable. Here is a proven path:

Face Reality
- There are new problems
- People will be different
- You will meet and be met with resistance – personal and from others
- Change is here – deal with it

Attitude – key to success
- Change is a test of your emotional resilience
- Remember attitude is also a by-product of habit and is a behavior

Focus on Goals
- Focus on a desired outcome
- Challenge those around you to help achieve the goal
- Ask for personal accountability

Communicate and Listen
- Practice empathy
- Validate the feelings being expressed by the other person
- Relay all necessary information right away to avoid gossip or conjecture
- Make sure all issues pertinent to the affected people are covered

Involve Skeptics
- The one who says "no" when given some measure of responsibility and recognition in the change process is likely to become a staunch supporter over time

Role Model
- Work with confidence
- Continue to communicate expectations
- Be scrupulous about walking your talk
- Admit when you've made a mistake
- Make positive choices

Work with a Sense of Urgency
- Set the pace
- Acknowledge those who match your enthusiasm and energy

Focus on the Need of the Customer
- Consider the positive impact the desired change can have for the customer
- Stop worrying about your turf and deal with the needs of your clients
- Understand that their needs are changing and evolving

Recognize and Reward Contributions
- Offer sincere gratitude
- Praise in Public

You are the Agent of Change

The facts:

Humans resist change because they fear it; it takes them out of their comfort zone.

You have things you can do to become an agent of change.

Make it personal. You are an integral part of your business. No organization wants to change for change's sake — they change to improve things, become more productive, enhance employee engagement, to achieve financial soundness, to produce a tangible result for the customer.

You will have greater ability to change because you practice risk-taking and strategic, actionable steps that allow you to expand and grow. You flex those expansion muscles and are a role model of growth to others.

You communicate in a way where people feel safe to try new things, mistakes are considered course correction, and learning is the norm.

Author and teacher Neale Donald Walsch said, "Life begins at the end of your comfort zone." That's when magic happens, when leadership expands.

Action Steps

1. Remember a time when you took a significant risk in your life. Maybe school, a relationship, a sky-dive, or whatever you did that jettisoned you out of your comfort zone.
   1. Journal about the experience and the feelings before, during, and after.
2. Think about something you currently desire or want to do but feel stuck and not able to execute.
   1. Journal about what it is, why it is important to you.
   2. Do a quick pros and cons list.
   3. Commit to one small action or behavior change that will create momentum.

5

THE DRAMA TRIANGLE - BEHAVIORS THAT CREATE DRAMA

Leadership vs. Dysfunctional Behavior

You aspire to be an effective leader. You've analyzed strengths and weaknesses and have made commitments to improve skill or leverage strength. You also have a keen understanding of several ways that you can rob yourself of your leadership by ignoring your commitment to emotional intelligence, indulging in triggers, or staying comfortable with the way things are.

When you live in "the way things are," you tip over into a series of dysfunctional relationships. These relationships reoccur continuously in any family or organization that has not made a conscious choice to do whatever it takes to take 100% responsibility as a leader. Some common behavioral archetypes are likely at the center of the comfort zone. These mental roadblocks are so comfortable that even though they are incredibly disruptive to your organization, you continually tolerate the familiar behavior – from yourself and others.

It's time to make a pledge to yourself: This stops now.

The descriptions you are about to read may sound uncomfortably familiar. Many transformational teachers talk about these behavioral types in one way or another. In the Leadership Mastery™ system, identifying these mental paradigms is part of a complete pivot into leadership, once they are fully understood.

First, let's look at the dreaded...

Drama Triangle

When you are triggered, under stress, or simply forget that you have the ability to make choices, you can be triggered into the never-never land of the dreaded Drama Triangle. This is where all leaders who run on auto-pilot or who have not made an appropriate choice end up.

The Drama Triangle is the dysfunctional behavior and thought processes that manifest themselves in three main characters: the Villain, the Victim, and the Hero. This is the antithesis of emotionally intelligent leadership.

> "Your suffering is never caused by the person you're blaming."
> - Byron Katie, author and teacher

Your suffering is never caused by the person you're blaming, the person you're saving, or the person you feel victimized by. Rather, you are suffering because of your thoughts about a person or situation. The way out has been set before you in the previous discussion regarding emotional intelligence and the management of your emotional triggers. Later in this chapter, you'll be given the secret equation that, when ruthlessly followed, will bounce you back into leadership on a dime!

The Drama Triangle of Villain, Victim, and Hero is a familiar pattern in both work, family, and community life. Historically, this human behavior dynamic was identified by Stephen Karpman as part of the transactional analysis field of study, but the archetypes are as old as time.

The Three Archetypes

Meet the Villain

The Villain likes to find problems. Once found, they like to blame people for them. The Villain shows up as bossy, critical, bullying, finger-pointing, and angry. They are the criticizer, the one who picks on you, the one who points out all the errors, the one who blames you, the one who shames you*, the one who makes you feel bad. The Villain's job is to find the problem, point out who is to blame for that problem, and make that person pay for creating the problem. Unwilling to take accountability for the situation, the Villain fails to realize many times they are contributors to the very problem they are criticizing. The Villain is teflon®, and the behavior you will observe is this person blaming the outside – YOU – for the problem. They are a heat-seeking problem finder with the finger of blame pointed at you. Every Villain needs the next character, the Victim, to pick on.

*A special word about blame and shame. When you are blamed, you are being faulted for behavior choices and when you are shamed, you are being faulted for being yourself. There is little that fries the brain more than shame. Demoralizing, belittling, and character-assassinating, shame will consume a person and they will end up doing stupid things and making life-decimating choices. Unless you are acting in totally unethical, amoral, and despicable ways, there is no reason to accept anyone's shame judgment on you. Find a way out and into leadership.

Meet the Victim

This archetype feels the world is against them and views it from a helpless and hopeless position. They feel that they are at the mercy of the actions and whims of others and have no perceived control of their environment. They say things like, "managers are evil," "money doesn't grow on trees," "I'm just unlucky," "you never taught me how to do it," "my [family/country/spouse/boss] won't let me do that," "why am I always being singled out?" You get the picture. The Victim feels powerless and unable to affect the situation. They expect to both be picked on and to be saved. Victims need Villains to reinforce their view that they are always in the one-down position. On the opposite side of the equation, the Victim needs the next archetype, the Hero, to remain helpless and in need of saving.

Meet the Hero

Trying to be of service in some way, the Hero swoops in to save the day, whether the day needs saving or not. They look for opportunities to be indispensable, to be the advice-giver, to fix things, to have all the answers. The motivating factor for the Hero is recognition for their heroic efforts. Many Heroes have a world belief that they must perform their duties because nobody can do it better. "If it's to be, it's up to me," is a popular albeit faulty statement. If you are reading this and have experienced a literal or virtual line out your door of advice-seekers, this archetype may resemble you. Heroes take action on behalf of others believing it's high service and not understanding the impact. If they do so much for others, the others are robbed of the opportunity to learn and do for themselves. All Heroes need both Victims and Villains as they are, indeed, the glue that holds the drama together.

Impact on Accountability

Can you see why this drama would have an impact on your culture of accountability? The Villain will never be accountable because the problem is always outside of themself; their job is merely to point their finger at it. The Victim will never be accountable because they don't have enough power to do so; they can't see what they might do to contribute to an outcome. The Hero has false accountability; their behavior might be first perceived as accountability, but really, they are just meddling, sticking their nose in places and situations that others could easily address.

How Does It Happen?

When you experience a triggering situation, it provokes an emotion or familiar behavior or thought pattern. You have to make a leadership choice at this juncture. That choice is to manage your emotions and behaviors. If you fail to do so, you are invited into the swirl of the Drama Triangle. If you make the behavior or communication choice typical for your "archetype of choice," you will defend and justify those actions that emanate from your trigger. You cement the thoughts, beliefs, paradigms, and behaviors that line up behind Villain, Victim, or Hero because you offer no alternative way to view the situation. This leads to justification and self-righteousness.

A Villain, triggered by discovering a problem or something that appears wrong to them, will justify their abusive behavior as a way of bringing attention to the problem. Because they see no alternative, such as questioning root causes or solving problems, they choose to blame and shame. Their behavioral choices become habits, and more and more problems present themselves. There is a universal tenet that says that what we focus on will be repeated. Justifying their blaming ways under the guise of eradicating problems, the cycle continues and continues.

The Victim is triggered when there is any perceived threat of being blamed or shamed in any way. They will also become triggered and defensive if they are asked to take on something that is unfamiliar to them or may cause them to have to own the result of their choices. Because they do not want to be in the spotlight of accountability, they are likely to complain, gossip, deflect, use false humility, or look for another Victim to take the fall for them. They may also look for a Rescuer to save the day for them. Just as the Villain feels justified in their behavioral choices so, too, does the Victim. "My gossip or complaint is completely justified because even the world is out to get me," goes their thinking. This becomes an endless cycle of self-confirming beliefs about their own disadvantaged position.

The Hero sees something left undone at every turn. They can identify when a Victim is being picked on or when a Villain is targeting someone, and this triggers their instinct to play the role of the Hero. They practice a distorted form of "stop, look, listen." Unfortunately, for those who like to rescue, this means "stop thinking, see things that are not there, and listen to my own voice of justification to save the day." They will speak for the Villain to try to soothe the ragged edges and they will problem solve for the Victim, offering advice or doing whatever task needs to be done themselves. In their rationale for their actions, there is usually a quid pro quo that is never fully stated but always bubbling below the surface. Their rationale goes, "I will fix this for you, save the day for you, be the one with all the answers for you… but you must acknowledge your need for me and praise me for my contribution." Heroes are trickier than the other two archetypes because their "service" may go unquestioned or unnoticed for years!

There was an old-time cartoon melodrama produced in the 1960's, *Dudley Do-Rite*. In the cartoon, the three archetypes were found in the main characters of Snidely Whiplash (Villain), Nell (Victim), and Dudley (Hero). Let's cue action...

Cast of Characters:

Snidely Whiplash – the nefarious, evil, bullying landowner and landlord to Nell

Nell – A helpless, hopeless, hapless young woman who simply cannot take care of herself

Dudley Do-Rite – A Canadian mounted police officer whose job in life is to rescue the beleaguered Nell

- Begin Scene - Action -

Nell (gnashing her teeth): "But I can't pay the rent."

Snidely (twisting his dastardly mustache): "But you must pay the rent!"

Nell (pulling out her trusty handkerchief to catch her precious tears): "But, I *can't* pay the rent..."

Snidely (flashing his grimacing smile): "But you must pay the rent! If you can't pay the rent, I will tie you up to the railroad and leave you there until you either pay the rent or the train comes."

(Snidely swoops Nell up and she helplessly kicks her feet and flails her arms until she nearly faints. Snidely cackles out his evil laugh as he takes her to the railroad and ties her to the rails.)

(From the mountaintop, we see a lone, noble figure on a horse, galloping down to the scene of the disaster. We hear the whistle of the train.)

Snidely (gnashing of teeth): "Oh drat! It's Dudley Do-Right of the Canadian Mounted Police!"

Dudley (galloping and flashing a pearly set of white teeth): "Don't worry, Nell. I'll save you."

(Dudley arrives, unties Nell in the nick of time)

Dudley (embracing Nell): "I'll pay the rent."

Nell (falling into Dudley's arms): "My hero."

Snidely (snapping his fingers): "Curses, foiled again!"

- End Scene -

It's very clear in this melodrama who is who. What about you? Which of the three archetypes resonates the most with you? Did any of these archetypes remind you of your own behavior? Did you identify one archetype in particular that you often revert to?

Can you be all three in one situation? Of course. Let's explore how.

It's easy to go around the bases of Villain, Victim, and Hero.

Let's draw from family life.

Jeanne is a single parent with teenagers. She mostly identifies in the Hero role and she has done a good job of teaching her family how to treat her. She does the shopping, plans the meals, does the laundry, pays the bills, etc.

Waking up one day, she wanders downstairs to find a sink full of dirty dishes for the fourth day in a row. She feels taken advantage of. The pivot to Victim begins. "Why am I the only one who does the dishes around here? Am I the maid? Nobody helps. I work hard. I deserve support."

Gathering a head of steam, she pivots to Villain. She takes her frustrations out on the family. "All you rotten kids," she screams, "get your butts out of bed and get downstairs. You are slobs. I can't believe you leave the dishes in the sink like this. Look at all the wasted food on the counter. Who do you think you are?!" The kids stumble down the stairs to the wild-eyed and furious woman before them. They are simply confused. After all, doesn't Mom always clean up the mess?

Looking at their sleepy and confused faces, she worries she has gone too far. Losing her Villain steam, she reverts back to Hero. "Whatever. (sigh) We'll just order pizza tonight and use paper plates that we can throw away."

Jeanne stays in this cycle – until she becomes conscious of her decisions. In her realization, she discovers that she can make a different choice. Rather than maintain the status quo, she can choose to allow natural consequences and then create agreements for different kinds of behavior for all involved. But she can't get there if she's stuck in this cycle. And neither can you.

The Scourge of the Hero

In corporate Leadership Mastery™ classes, most of the participants self-identify as the Hero. Everyone wants to be helpful and supportive to others. It is part of our mental wiring as humans. They are surprised to learn that the Hero is, in fact, the most harmful of the three. When does helpfulness mask a need for control? When is attention to detail a disguise for a desire to be the smartest person in the room?

Ego is a sneaky little thing. It often disguises itself as doing good for others. What looks noble on the outside is self-serving on the inside.

■ ■ ■

Personal Perspective

I'd like to share a personal story about how sneaky "being helpful" can be.

A few months ago, I made a new connection. We had a great conversation about how this person is expanding into a new venture. She asked me to participate as a guest on her radio show and I happily agreed. I could tell that our purpose and values were in alignment and that we could be of mutual support to each other.

Towards the end of our chat, I began to offer my network connections. I could hear my voice saying, "I'm pretty well-connected in this field, and I'd be happy to refer others to your new adventure." I immediately felt defense from the other side. I was confused.

On the surface, my offer appeared innocent and charitable. However, something else was really going on. Look at the opening line: "I'm pretty well-connected in this field." That was my ego saying, "I'm important and you should listen to me and learn from me." This is all wrapped up in a socially acceptable way of being helpful. Let's look under the hood for more information.

My new friend got triggered and began to defend the depth of her own network. At first, I couldn't understand her defensiveness. Upon examination, I had to own my side of the issue. *I had sent an ego stealth missile into the conversation and created a culture of competition rather than collaboration.* I guess if I dug deep enough, I would've made the connection between the way my personality felt threatened to the way my ego sent the message, "it's time for the competition." The real lesson for me was how I inserted my "helpfulness" into the conversation and eroded respect.

My experience is a warning call. Be wary of your need to be helpful. First, your version of help is not necessarily needed. Second, your version of help may be more about control than service.

What if we did a redo? What if I went back into that conversation and instead said, "How useful would it be to you to have additional resources in your network as you launch?" It's a question. It allows the other person to decide if help or support is needed or desired. That creates reciprocity in the relationship and it's respectful.

■ ■ ■

Being overly and unnecessarily helpful is an unconscious patterning of behavior that repeats over time. This "helpful" thing is a petri dish of awareness.

Be careful of helpful…it's like its 4-letter word cousin, "Nice." On the surface, the urge to help others seems altruistic, useful, and benevolent. Underneath this appearance, however, your motives may be less than pure.

The Way Out

Here it is. The secret equation that was promised to you. Culled from the genius vault that is Jack Canfield's *Success Principles*, the Leadership Formula is a recipe for leadership success.

The only way out is E+R=O – which stands for Event + Response/Reaction = Outcome.

It goes like this.

- Something happens, a situation occurs, and you are in the Event.
- From the Event, you will eventually get an Outcome.

- That outcome is deeply impacted by the way you manage the "R" part of the equation. Will you react or will you respond? Think back to the earlier chapter on triggers. This "R" is at the heart of that.

The way into leadership is to take a deep breath, choose to respond, and be wary of knee-jerk reactions. Manage the "R" by remembering your strategies for managing emotional triggers and make a choice that puts you into leadership. Even if you achieve an undesirable outcome, remaining calm and deliberate in your decision-making will help you to feel empowered and enabled.

When you are empowered and enabled, you will be equipped to support the archetype transformation from dysfunction to leadership.

The Archetype Transformation

In *The Empowerment Dynamic*, author David Emerald suggests that we shift the view of the three archetypes. Loosely borrowing from his idea, here is a leadership transformation path for Villain, Victim, and Hero.

Villain to Quality Control

The Villain has a more palatable purpose than beating people up for any perceived mistakes they've made. The Villain, at their heart, truly sees a problem or a flaw and is committed to the flaw being recognized. The Villain is often hung up on their own flaws and fears but would do anything to not be found out.

What if you were to recast this character as an agent of quality control? This recasting permits the former Villain to notice when things are incorrect and to not only call attention to them (without blaming others), but also to participate in the plan to fix it. This still gives them the measure of control that they long for, but puts it to greater purpose.

When you notice another acting out the role of the Villain, you have an opportunity to ask powerful open-ended questions that would create more functional behavior of problem solving and quality control.

For example:

- How well do you understand the problem?
- How would you solve the issue?
- How do you prevent this in the future?
- How could you communicate the issue to create collaboration for the solution?

Victim to Activator

The Victim, who is unable to see how to have an impact, can be recast as an activator. When the drama of Victimhood is removed, what remains is a deep need to be safe and create safety for others. As you are working with someone stuck in the Victim archetype, remember they have a need to feel safe which makes them shy away from resolutions or accountability. This individual needs to be taught how to handle challenges, make decisions, and create a little momentum.

The new framework is setting expectations, communicating boundaries, saying no, and acting on the power of small action. Help former Victims create small victories that add up.

Some appropriate coaching questions might sound like:

- What's one thing you could change?
- What would help you to feel more in control?
- What is one action you can take to improve the situation?
- How would you solve the problem?

Hero to Catalyst

The Hero, in their dysfunction, is service to others gone awry. There is a combination of inner desire of control and service. If they can control the situation by being the main provider of service to others, all is well. This becomes problematic when their need to provide service flies in the face of another's desire for independence and autonomy. When the Hero is unconscious and lacks self-awareness, they rob those around them of their autonomy and ability to learn through experience. The hard thing here is that often Heroes are often smart individuals. They do see the lay of the land and immediately see the hole to fill or the knowledge that's needed. They just don't have the discretionary muscles to wait it out to see if others step up to the plate, nor the leadership oomph to call another forward to the plate.

How do you help the Hero make better leadership decisions? Help them to move from Hero to Catalyst. Here's the pivot into leadership. At 30,000 feet in the air with wisdom and attention, the Catalyst sees the spark which is needed and then asks great questions, bumping people back to their own wisdom and knowledge. The Catalyst participates in eliciting positive outcomes – *through others*.

Here's how you might coach a Hero through their own transformation into a Catalyst:

- How can we use this problem to develop more problem solvers?
- Who can you delegate to?
- Who on the team needs an opportunity to learn?
- What would happen if you were not available to solve this issue?

Support Your Personal Transformation

Thus far, you've been focusing on how to support transformation in other people. What about yourself?

You've diagnosed your own personal archetype(s) when triggered. Go back and review what has been written about supporting others and know that every bit of it can be personalized for your own transformation.

The great coaching questions that can bring others from Villain to Quality Control, from Victim to Activator, and from Hero to Catalyst are also effective self-coaching questions.

Here are a few more ideas that might support you:

- Learn to pay attention instead of relying on your automatic responses. The automatic responses are found within your comfort zone. The attention is found in risk-taking.

- When you do pay attention, you become self-aware and are better able to take full responsibility for what's troubling you. Don't blame somebody else, don't try to fix somebody else, figure out what's going on for you.
- Your awareness enables you to better assess how you created or fueled the situation. It wouldn't be happening "to you" if you were not participating.
- Explore the underlying familiar pattern for the triggers that propel you into one of the three Drama Triangle characters. When you get to the root of the trigger and feel all your feelings wrapped up in that familiar place, it loses its power over you.
- Express your feelings without blaming other people. They're just feelings, and they are yours.
- Shift into curiosity about how you can create something different.
- Brainstorm all solutions, no matter how silly or grandiose or impractical they may seem.
- Decide on some new behaviors or commit to a different solution and then keep your commitments to the solutions.

These actions will permit you to go beyond where you typically get stuck and move into your most authentic self, which is that wonderful, emotionally-intelligent leader that is inside of you.

THOUGHTFUL ACTION

The beautiful thing about most actions or decisions in life is that you can always redo them. Perhaps you redo them with the person in the moment and change the entire situation on a dime. Other times, you will practice a redo in your mind. Avoid self-recrimination by allowing the redo to teach you something new. Try this exercise.

The Drama Triangle to Empowerment Triangle

Three common reactions will play out in a conflicted, stressed situation or when confronted with a habitual pattern/trigger. The Villain is the nefarious bad guy; the Hero is the action-oriented good guy; the Victim is the innocent sufferer who is acted upon negatively by others.

Think about a recent interaction/situation where you showed up in one of the archetypes. Use the E+R=O formula to diagnose the actual situation and to envision a preferred response and outcome.

Specifically, remember a time when you were one of these characters. What EVENT sparked your REACTION which gave you what OUTCOME?

If you could go back in time and redo the situation, what would you do differently? You would still have the EVENT. This time you would choose to manage your trigger and RESPOND versus react. What different OUTCOME might you envision?

Remember your character options:

Villain: Categorized by scanning for negatives, blaming others, adrenaline rush with problems. Positive Intention: To solve problems. To help the world in some way.

Victim: Categorized by feeling sorry for self, asking "why me," feeling powerless. Positive Intention: Desire to be safe and create a different story.

Hero: Categorized by being helpful, expedient, having the answers and swooping in to save the day. Positive Intention: By helping others and stopping the villain, she is demonstrating devotion to the common good and can be a catalyst for positive change.

Try It:

- Use this grid to remember a time you acted as a Villain, Victim, or Hero
- Write down the event that occurred in the "what happened" column
- Write down your REACTION
- Write down your Outcome
- Do the Redo by writing down the exact same event

- Imagine and write a different RESPONSE
- Predict a new or better outcome

	What Happened	The Redo
Event		
R		
Outcome		

Based upon what I have discovered, what is one commitment I am willing to make?

In Summary

The Drama Triangle is as old as time. Your participation is likely muscle memory from childhood. The good news is that awareness creates an opportunity for change. As you become more and more aware of how this shows up for you personally, as well as in your communities, you can make different choices. You can turn excuse-making into positive forward action. You can turn blaming into root cause analysis for problem solving. You can turn your rescuing into coaching for performance.

With this, you emerge as an empowered leader. Your emotional intelligence is required to bust through this triangle. As you become more adept, you create environments where drama is minimized, trust is elevated, and performance hums!

Action Steps

1. Self-identify. Are you more prone to Villain, Victim, or Hero behaviors when stressed?
   1. Observe your own reactions and behaviors for a week
   2. Identify the behaviors you exhibit when in each of the characters
   3. Notice whether a shift occurs with your awareness
2. Complete the Redo exercise above and begin to understand the shift from reaction to response and its impact on your behavior choices.
3. Teach another about the Drama Triangle so that you have a partner to brainstorm (and come clean) with.

PHASE II
COMMUNICATION
LEADERSHIP

At the heart of the humanized leader is the ability to communicate. The team member who is fully listened to, the client who clearly understands terms, and the feedback that creates performance improvement are the key leadership skills that change businesses and, indeed, worlds.

The last section encouraged you to lead through emotions. This section incorporates all of that learning and insists that you emerge as an impeccable communicator.

Let's go!

6

THE HE(ART) OF COMMUNICATION

Friends Tell the Truth: From the Mary Pat Archives

I have a sassy, wonderful friend, Lee. She has been a great teacher for me, and you will find her fingerprints all over this book. During my own leadership development that I call the "know-it-all" phase, Lee gently reminded me of the importance of listening first. She looked at me and said, "Two big ears and one small mouth, my dear." This loving admonition has been with me ever since.

Caring and Curiosity

Communication is rich and effective when people are assured you have their best interests at heart.

Communication that is wrapped up in the qualities of caring and curiosity is the best kind of EQ communication. Caring means that I suspend my need to be first, loudest, and most important and instead include or yield to you. Curiosity

> *"People don't care how much you know until they know how much you care."*
>
> – Theodore Roosevelt, 26th President of The United States

means that I genuinely want to know what is on your mind and why you think the way you do or make the choices that you do. This is not to evaluate or find fault but to connect and build relationships.

These qualities create the highest levels of trust.

There are two leadership skills that will create this kind of trust: listening and asking questions.

Listen!

The singular people-connecting skill that any leader must master is the skill of listening but not just any kind of listening. Leaders must listen with their whole being. There is so much riding on the skill of listening – from your employees feeling heard and validated to obtaining key information to drive the business objectives. It is the key skill of emotionally intelligent leadership.

It pays to listen, and it pays to listen well.

If you are like most, you think you are a good listener. You are probably not as good as you think you are.

All kinds of human things get in the way of listening in a whole-hearted way. They could be perceptions of time, your need to reply, a desire to fix the situation, disinterest, or any other array of conditions that thwart your willingness and even your ability to listen fully.

Whole-hearted listening up-levels the conversation. Whole-hearted listening is a body, mind, and heart thing.

What does this look like in practice? Read on. Let's look at the ingredients to let you listen with your whole heart and mind.

Listen with Your Body – Be involved physically. As you settle into your body and ground yourself in the here and now, you will feel relaxed. There is a greater willingness to really look at the other person, nod, and make eye contact. As an emotionally intelligent leader, you are also attuned to how your body responds to the stimuli and what you hear. This physical presence creates safety for the conversation and gives you some additional information as you settle in to observe.

Listen with Your Mind – Permit your mind to quiet so that you can be present in the conversation. When your mind is jumping around, you will miss the meat of what is being said and what is intended. Quit mentally rehearsing your reply. Listen to make connections. Use your intellect to create a mind map of what the person is truly saying to you. Be mindful and smart enough to allow the person to come to their own conclusions.

Listen with Your Heart – Be involved emotionally. This is not about caretaking, but about caring. Let your intuition guide your open-ended questions. Engaging your heart to be here now and no place else will help your mind and body grow quiet so that you can be at ease offering heart-to-heart, respectful attention. Empathize and have compassion but avoid the conversation takeover that often happens out of discomfort or the desire to fix things.

Be easy about this. Listening, like leadership, is presence, not performance. Witnessing and compassionate presence is what is required. When you "try" to listen, resistance and effort is introduced. Simply allowing yourself to listen is effortless and time stands still – for both parties. That kind of listening is deeply fulfilling.

Listening is a skill that must be practiced. Compare it to learning to lift weights. Both are mastered with repetition. Silence, listening for themes, paraphrasing, asking open-ended questions, using a pause, and body language are all basic, practiced skills.

When you listen better, you lead better. When you lead better, the team performs better. Win. Win. Win.

You will acquire a more whole-hearted way of listening if you pay attention and practice these five cues:

1. Encourage others to express issues and feelings
    -   What you might say: "I want to know," "please tell me," or "how did that feel?"
    -   This adds richness to the conversation as emotions create another level of exchange. It also shows respect and caring.

2. Clarify
   - What you might say: "Can you say more?" "Did I hear you say...?"
   - Not only do you want to make sure you are tracking the conversation, you may intuit that there is something left unsaid and the clarification may surface that.

3. Restate/Label
   - What you might say: "It sounds like..." or "It appears that..."
   - Loosely borrowed from author/negotiator, Chris Voss (*Never Split the Difference*), this allows you to do two things at once. Firstly, you can restate the facts as you understand them. Secondly, this is an opportunity to check out your assumptions about what the other person is saying. If you have labeled them incorrectly, the other person will have the opportunity to clarify.

4. Reflect Feelings
   - What you might say: "I can imagine how..."; "It seems like you were angry..."; "I can tell how frustrated you are."
   - This is a kissing cousin to restating/labeling and different from point one (which is a general stance of encouraging the validation of issues). Here is the opportunity to be completely in the moment and reflect the feelings that you are hearing and feeling from the other person. You may be right or wrong, yet offering this reflection allows the other person to say yes or no and takes the conversation to a new place.

5. Validate and Appreciate
   - What you might say: "I'm happy we talked," "I'm glad we are trying to figure this out," or "I appreciate knowing about this."
   - This is the maraschino cherry on top of the sundae. This one closing of a conversation, delivered in real-time and with complete sincerity, buttons up the safety and sacredness of the listening and sharing that just occurred. This is not about agreeing with what you just heard – you may or

may not agree. This is about honoring that people want to be acknowledged and appreciated. Your time spent listening coupled with your validation creates expansion and – yes – love.

It takes courage to be a whole-hearted listener just as it takes courage to be in the spotlight of leadership. Courage and vulnerability don't need to be hard. When body, mind, and heart are part of the equation, you are supported. Things can be easier, more grounded, intentional yet effortless. Bonus: you are more accessible to your people, you can connect in a masterful way, and you get priceless information that strengthens the bond.

What is more true in this day and age of rapid-fire information is that you have stopped listening.

Here is the current situation and you can be a part of changing the trajectory. It's apparent everywhere you turn. The media screams, the White House screams, the streets scream, and – in your face all the time – social media screams.

It's already been established that one of the greatest gifts given to another is to listen. You create connection and meaning. You offer and receive a gift. The one being listened to receives the gift of acknowledgement, recognition, and attention. The one doing the listening receives wisdom, information, and peace.

Listening is the key to making decisions, to solving problems, to changing all those things we are shouting about.

Why don't people do it very well?

Client after client and student after student have demonstrated that it isn't done well because the moment another person starts talking, you have already begun to prepare your response. You stop being still, being curious, being connected and begin being in charge again, trying to control outcomes. The 'listen to speak' model neglects two important components in the listening process:

1. Understanding the message
2. Interpreting through a filter cleared of your assumptions and judgments

Here's an acronym that brings the process into clear light: H U I R

H – Hearing
- The physical act of sensing sound

U – Understanding
- The realization that someone is offering a message or theme

I – Interpreting
- How you hear it based upon your assumptions, biases, experience, or ego

R – Responding
- What you will say based upon what you have heard, understood, and interpreted

If you are honest with yourself, you are likely to jump directly from H to R and skip the understanding and interpreting. As you prepare your response to the noise you have heard, you forget to listen to understand fully what is being said. What's the undercurrent? What emotion is being expressed? What's slipping between the lines? If you are communicating in-person, what body language are you noticing?

You may neglect to interpret correctly. Interpreting means that you have suspended your judgments and assumptions. You suspend what you think you know about what is being said. You clean your filter with the cleanser of curiosity. Interpretation relies on you having a clean leadership filter. If your leadership filter is clogged up with comfort zone behaviors or old beliefs and paradigms or judgments and assumptions about the person who's speaking, your interpretation will be off and you will never arrive at the proper response.

When you do respond, you must honor the emotion and pay attention to the facts. Going for the jugular of the problem puts you into "fixing mode," and you've seen how that turns out in the Drama Triangle! Acknowledge or honor the emotion and then state the facts as you have understood them.

"I can tell how passionate you feel about this. Let's make sure I have the facts clear."

Many fool themselves into believing they are great listeners. Be willing to be Zen about this. In other words, approach listening with a beginner's mind.

Four Ways You Can Up Your Game

- **Practice silence.** Your attention is like a prayer. Breathe deeply, become curious, be willing to suspend your agenda, and sit quietly to allow the other person all the time they need. How do you feel during times of extended silence? Do you start giggling like a kid who is supposed to be quiet during the school assembly? Do you want to fill in the gaps? Do you want to be "helpful" and provide the answer to the other person? Be aware how you feel in times of silence in the presence of other people and practice.
- **Attend.** How you sit, using eye contact (or not), head nodding, and using gentle non-verbal words are all ways of attending. Attending is about body language and your presence. Are you involved in the conversation? Can your partner recognize your involvement? Stay present, pay attention to the conversation, and demonstrate this presence with both body and energy.
- **Pay attention and honor emotion.** Often what's being said is more purely communicated in the emotions being expressed than the words being uttered. A great leader who is also a great listener will pay attention to two things during a conversation: feeling and fact. If you can reflect the speaker's emotions and clarify the facts in what they're saying, you have created connection and validation.
- **Respond versus React.** Remember the E+R=O formula from the Drama Triangle? Pay attention to your own emotions as a listener. When we give in to the impulse of reaction, that's when we jump in with our own agenda. Take a few deep breaths and stay with the conversation.

Listening As It Applies to the Leader/Employee One-on-One

What ratio of listening to talking is appropriate for regular meetings with a direct report in a scheduled one-on-one?

You would do well to actively employ an 80/20 ratio during a one-on-one. That's you spending 80% of your time listening and 20%

of your time talking. One way to ensure you maintain this ratio is to encourage your employee to set the meeting agenda, rather than you. Ask a few key questions to get the ball rolling, then actively participate by listening well.

So that you do not think that listening is passive, let's be clear.

> "Effective questioning brings insight, which fuels curiosity, which cultivates wisdom."
>
> – Chip Bell

Listening is active and alive and alert. When you listen and listen well, you are easily able to create meaningful dialogue with the other, moving beyond the surface. That's when the magic happens. If you were ever in love, this will be familiar. You hung on every word but there was nothing inactive in you. You felt alive and connected and deeply curious. Maybe listening is a lot like love!

Listening deeply allows us to create new possibilities and seek common ground, rather than *"my ground."* The world is depending upon our willingness to upgrade this skill.

Let's start listening…

Maybe you'd like to know how you stack up as a leader who listens. If so, download the listening assessment here: www.thehumanized-leader.com/Bonus

Curiosity – The Power of the Question

Listening becomes super-charged when you employ the skill of asking the open-ended question.

You might be thinking, "What does a question have to do with listening?" I mean, after all, don't they require two different intentions, much less two different body parts?

A well-placed question is the hidden treasure of good listening. It invites your communicating partner or partners to open up, open a new door, find a new path to deepen the conversation.

In its simplest form, there are two types of questions – open-ended and closed-looped.

The Close Looped Question

The close-looped questions are those that elicit a yes or no answer. Do I turn here? Is this information correct? Do you agree? They are best suited to find out information, clarify an issue, and find out basic directional information. Where they go astray is when leaders use them to bring people back to their own assumptions, biases, and conclusions. You have a point of view and don't even realize that you are asking leading questions to bring your listeners into agreement with you. This is how you close a conversation, stop listening, and signal to others that the conversation is not open any more. Use care with your closed-loop questions.

The Open-Ended Question

The optimal question is the open-ended question. As the name implies, it keeps the communication loop open and evolving. These are questions that invite a deepening of the sharing that occurs during conversation and expand your ability to listen more fully.

"Who, what, where, when, why, how" are your cues. Michael Bungay Stanier, in *The Coaching Habit*, adds another key question for your arsenal when he asks, "and what else?"

You can also try an invitational command, such as "Tell me more."

A key to an effective open-ended question can be in how you elicit feelings. Simply asking questions – such as "How did you feel?" or "How did that make you feel?" or "How do you feel about…?" – can be an effective way of connecting your communicator to their feelings. Try it another way to connect them to understanding empathetically the feelings of others.

Ask meaningful and open-ended questions as this encourages the speaker to clarify and continue. Remember that open-ended questions always leave the door open for more conversation and information. Ask a "who, why, what, where, when, how" question and then, in the words of *Fierce Conversations* author, Susan Scott, "Let silence do the heavy lifting."

A note on yes or no questions: Become aware of the patterns that emerge when asking closed-ended questions. Sometimes you ask yes or no questions to check off a box on your agenda. You may be wanting to obtain agreement or lead people to see things your way through yes or no questions.

Opening Up the Question

You may find open-ended questions difficult. You are in good company. Most leaders took their place as they moved swiftly and expediently up the ladder. Direction, decisions, and action plans were the rule. That expediency favors the closed question or outright statement. Your open-ended question muscles are weak.

The best way to tune into open-ended questions is to practice using the following prompts: who, what, where, when, why, how, and what else, tell me more, and tell me about.

Use the following list as a primer. Consider the closed question and brainstorm as many ways that you can "open the question up."

Did you go to the meeting?	Ex. What was decided at the meeting?
Do you understand?	Ex. What additional information do you need?
Did you review the specs?	Ex. How do the specs comport to our abilities?
Did you talk with him?	Ex. Tell me more about your discussion.
Are you doing better?	Ex. How are you feeling today?
Can you finish on time?	Ex. What might get in the way of timely completion?

Be Wary of the Harmful Question

As a leader, you must be on to yourself and understand your own motivations and intentions. You may think you are asking open-ended questions, when in reality you have begun an interrogation. Open-ended questions can become harmful when they devolve into accusation, finger-pointing, or fault-finding. The "why" question, as effective as it may be for diagnosis, will become harmful in a conflicted conversation or a feedback conversation if it is received as accusatory. "Why did you do that?" can feel like an attack. What questions might you use instead, even if they involve more language? How about, "Tell me the steps you took," or "How did you arrive at your decision(s)?" or "How do you feel about your result?" It may be a longer road of communication, but it will be more inviting – and you will get the real information you need.

A similar harmful question can begin with "what." "What were you thinking?" can be received as a direct critical hit. Why not try, "How did you decide on the outcome?" or "What was your thought process?" or another variation that indicates your curiosity and not your condemnation.

Back to the Magical Leadership Elixir: Curiosity

People are complex and you encounter all types of people with all their various histories, intentions, motivations, and family upbringings. You simply cannot fully know what makes another person tick or what they are truly and deeply thinking – unless...you create emotional safety for them with a true, honest, and deep commitment to curiosity.

Curiosity invites silence. There is a dance that happens between the silence and space of listening and the clarification or curiosity of a great question. When you are deeply listening to someone, another part of your brain turns on and you will intuitively know when to be of service with a great question. Keep your agenda at bay.

> *Being* heard is *so close to being loved* that for the average person, they are almost indistinguishable.
>
> – David W. Augsburger, Author and Pastoral Counselor

Action Steps

1. Make a list of all of the ways that block your ability to listen well (ie. distractions, not interested, forming my own response...).
2. Select one from your list to improve each week for the next month (4 different improvements).
3. Notice when you ask yes/no or leading questions and practice pivoting to open-ended questions.
4. Question your motivations, habits, or beliefs with your yes/no questions.
5. Use the Drama Triangle transformations by noticing Villain, Victim, or Hero behaviors in yourself or others.
6. Notice the archetype.
7. Use open questions to move the Villain to quality control, Victim to creator, and Hero to coach/mentor.

7

CUSTOMIZE COMMUNICATION TO MEET PEOPLE WHERE THEY ARE

Did you know that all people have an automatic pattern of how they communicate? It's called default communication behavior. When you are not aware or not actively looking to influence or connect, you just show up the way you are.

However, your default communication style may not get you what you desire. This is especially true when your style is diametrically opposed to another's. Communication is not a one-way street.

You are a bridge.

As an emotionally intelligent leader, able to navigate emotions and needs, you provide a bridge to those who have diverse styles of communicating. You know how to meet people on their side of the communication bridge. At one end of the bridge with another on the far side, the message needs to be sent in a way that the other person can understand. You may be tempted to communicate your message only from your style. If so, you may be only partially across the bridge as a good number of people receive information in a different manner than the way you're communicating. The world needs your message; let's make sure you are heard.

Communication is behavior and behavior is observable, situational, flexible, dynamic, and based on your thoughts and beliefs. That means communication can change by your own conscious choice.

Think about the diversity of communication and its impact on how you do or don't get along with certain people. If you were to make a list of people who were easy to be with and people who were difficult to be with, it would be apparent that the people who are easy to be with are similar and those more difficult to be with are different from you. Your styles are similar or different and when you don't know how to shift your style to ensure effective dialogue, miscommunication can be the result.

The Four Behavioral Styles

There are a multitude of behavioral styles which measure many different facets of communication, aptitude, and behavior. For the sake of simplicity, let's morph all the many behavioral profile results and distill them down to four common behavioral communication styles. You will be able to recognize yourself and others in your work and life as we discuss each.

Pretend you've drawn a cross in the middle of the page. At the top, imagine the word "outgoing" and on the bottom, place the word "reserved." On the left side of the page, write "task-oriented" and to the right side, write "people-oriented." This is the slice and dice in which we place the four different styles of communication. The variety of ways people show up fits within the matrix. Some are outgoing while committed to completing the task. Others are reserved yet like to get

things done through people. Which one is best? None are better than the others; they simply exist. They are ways that you are wired and show up, and all four parts of the matrix are absolutely needed and invaluable in running a business.

One style of communicator is the Driver, whose goal is to get things done. The Driver is task-oriented and outgoing, driving an agenda, and making things happen all through focus upon task completion. They see the world as filled with problems that need to be resolved. They easily take risks and move rapidly.

A second style is the Seller, whose goal is to receive appreciation (as in the sale or leadership). The Seller is outgoing and enjoys being in the spotlight and being at the front of the class. Naturally people-oriented, they want to be with the team but in the spotlight of leadership. They are verbal and often charismatic. Relationships are important to them so they will accomplish their tasks through people.

The third style is the Analyzer, whose goal is to make sure things are done correctly with data to back it up. Reserved and task-focused, they don't need nor do they want to be in the spotlight. They are too busy focusing on getting tasks accomplished by analyzing facts and data and historical information. They ask, "Why?" and make certain that key corporate metrics are achieved correctly. They avoid conflict and look at the world through the prism of standards.

The final style is the Team Player, whose goal is to have the team get along and win together. You may find these folks to be reserved, yet people-centric. Often described as "wind beneath the wings," they're committed to making sure that the team wins together. These types are like an anchor and they accomplish tasks with stability and harmony and don't like change.

With that cursory description, can you guess who you are? Are you a driver? Are you a seller? Are you an analyzer or are you a team player? It doesn't make any difference which of the many behavioral assessments you may have taken, you're generally going to fall into one or two of these four styles.

Pick Up the Clues and Customize

Now that you've seen all four of these types, what does it mean for you? Take what you see about yourself and then pick up the clues on the behaviors of others and customize your leadership communication. Each guest, client, and associate is unique, and they all have a preferred method of communicating. Without conscious thought, most selling or managing is based upon the behavioral style of the seller or the manager. If you truly are the bridge for communication, you will see that this is backwards. Know thyself and adapt to serve the person on the other side of the bridge.

Conflicts in style can result in tension, discomfort, and lost opportunities, so adapting your approach to the needs of the others will improve your chances of collaboration and results. Simple as that.

Let's Look at an Example

Adam has a natural tendency to appreciate details. He researches, knows his facts, can produce tables, and reasons. He is asked to lead a small team to roll out a new sales tracking system. Adam would like to advance his career with this company and sees this as an opportunity to produce great results and shine as a leader.

Cathy, his boss, makes quick decisions. She sees the long-term view, intuitively understands the obstacles, and works swiftly for immediate results. She delegates the detailed plans to her team so that she can continue to focus on longer-range plans and opportunities.

Adam, armed with all his facts and figures and the detailed research to back up the recommendation he is about to make, schedules a meeting with Cathy.

Can you see where this is heading? Adam, so proud of the data, takes Cathy through a winding road of factoids. He fails to notice her impatience or growing distracted behavior. The meeting does not go as he intended, and Cathy mandates a different choice. Cathy may feel like the situation is resolved, but Adam feels frustrated at the result.

Conflicts in communication styles can result in tension, discomfort, and lost opportunities.

Each guest, client, associate, or supervisor is unique and has a preferred method of doing business. Most people sell or manage based upon their own style, their own preference. That's not leading – it's managing. It doesn't get you what you desire, most of the time.

What if Adam had adapted his approach to Cathy? Adjusting your approach to how others prefer to be communicated with greatly improves the chances of collaboration and results. This is a key skill in emotional intelligence.

If you have high emotional intelligence you can recognize your own emotional state and the emotional states of others and engage with people in a way that draws them to you. You can understand your own communication style and the preferences of others. You use this understanding to better relate to others – customizing your style to theirs.

Let's Give Adam and Cathy a Do-over

Cathy has delegated a key opportunity to Adam, knowing that his eye for detail and commitment to the data will create an excellent and well thought-out solution.

Adam, appreciating Cathy's bottom line approach, creates a one-page executive summary to bring focus to the meeting.

Adam (with backup detail at the ready) presents the Executive Summary to Cathy. Cathy asks for some level of detail. Both are on the same page with discovery and recommendations and collaboration is possible. A decision is made, and both move forward with a desired outcome. Cathy got her bottom line and Adam shared the pertinent details.

Put It into Action

- <u>Recognize your responsibility</u> to create the bridge so that your message is received
- <u>Understand</u> where you fit in the behavioral matrix and how you prefer to communicate
- <u>Pick up the clues</u> from those around you to determine their preferences
- <u>Adjust your style</u> to meet their needs
  - Bottom line for drivers
  - Create connection with sellers
  - Provide details and data to analyzers
  - Create a clear playing field for team players
- <u>Rinse and repeat</u> until this all feels natural to you

The Ideal Leadership Team

There is a distinct benefit of having all four styles on the team. The ideal leadership team is a mixture of all four styles.

The Driver generates the ideas and insists on the results.

The Seller goes out to promote the ideas and generates the enthusiasm.

The Team Player makes certain that ideas are carried out and brings stability to the group.

The Analyzer makes certain that key details are covered and that the project is done well.

You need all four. Drivers, Sellers, Team Players, and Analyzers complete the puzzle. You will lead best when you customize your communication style to meet all four of the styles.

Emotional intelligence is strengthened with practice and consciousness. The idea of communication diversity creates an expanded playing field for the EQ leader and, in turn, creates a diverse customer service experience, stakeholder experience, and employee experience. It pays dividends to customize your communication.

Your ability to customize communication will have profound effects, including:

- Strengthening of trust and credibility
- Increased cooperation and innovation
- Ability to address and correct communication breakdowns
- Gaining more influence in both your life and work

When you know what your default style is and you know both the triggers and preferences of the other styles, you can be thoughtful and proactive in your approaches.

The result is getting what you need and strengthening your relationships without the communication road bumps.

Action Steps

1. Assess your own behavioral communication style. Why did you select this style?
2. Assess the behavioral communication style for each member of your team.
3. How does each person prefer to receive communication?
4. Practice, practice, practice.

8

FEEDBACK IS A GIFT

Introduction

Feedback is a gift, no matter how it's wrapped. It might be wrapped in a ragged brown paper bag or wrapped in shiny silver paper with a bow. Your secret gift can be hidden underneath crumpled and worn out tissue. No matter the packaging, it is a gift and when you receive the gift, your job is to find out what is inside for you.

Many leaders find feedback uncomfortable. This leads them to push harder or to avoid altogether.

A common motivation of a boss about to offer feedback is, "How do I make my employees change?" The employee's behavior (or the employee, themself) is an obstacle between the boss and their goal. Feedback becomes expedient – a way to make someone change so that you can get what you want. It's a set up.

Add to that, you may not have had the best role models for effective feedback. It's likely that your boss is not great at it, either.

This is an opportunity to change all of that. What if your feedback was healthy and offered in the spirit of improvement? How would you feel if your feedback supported others in their development and creation of success?

A person on the receiving end of healthy feedback is motivated to listen and perhaps change. Perhaps defensive at first, they feel supported. They understand that your feedback is coming from a good place.

It's time to take the onus off feedback as a way to control, punish, or criticize and put it in its proper place as a development tool.

Let's go.

Criticism or Feedback

What's the difference between criticism and feedback?

Criticism attacks. What's more, it attacks the person. It's sneaky as it disguises itself as trying to keep the other person safe – think of critical parents. It is more about controlling the other person so that the criticizer can stay in their own comfort zone.

Criticism attacks the person, not the behavior. "You always," "you never," "you should," "you ought to" are all trigger words that feed criticism. Think how often you use those phrases on yourself when you want to beat up on yourself or when you feel shame. Those phrases are familiar emotional hijacks, taking you right back into a small place of shame, blame, and humiliation.

Criticism is always about the person who is lobbing it. It's about their fear (even if the fear is for your situation), their opinion, their need for you to change to their preference. Ego-based, it does not factor in your feelings, desires, or how you need to be communicated to. Rather, it imposes a judgement on you, your character, or your choices.

Criticism is not feedback.

Feedback is always offered in the spirit of improvement. It focuses on behavior, not personality. It hones you in on actions you can take, thoughts you can have, attitudes you can acquire that lead you to successful outcomes. It does not come out of the blue, but rather is based on a behavior that is not serving you or the expectations you need to achieve.

If you believe that perceived failures are learning opportunities, then feedback creates a learning process rather than a mechanism to point out mistakes. Drop the Villain and move to Quality Control. Again, this is about *creating a learning process*. If you make a mistake, you simply course correct. It's a navigational tool that says that when you go off course, the feedback discussion will help you find a way back.

When communicating your feedback, there are four magical words that keep you in leadership:

Factual
- Dealing in fact and observable behavior allows the other to see what can be shifted or changed. Your opinion doesn't count (sorry!).

Direct
- Sometimes in discomfort, people will step too delicately around what needs to be said. The leader's job is to speak clearly and directly about the situation so the other is clear.

Neutral
- It is important that you clean your filter (made of your perceptions, biases, judgments, or assumptions) before offering feedback. If not, your feedback may be delivered as criticism. This is where trigger management is useful.

Kind
- Frustration or discomfort might cause you to be brusque. Mismanaged emotions may erupt as anger. It is important to remain kind. Mistakes, even those willful ones, do not deserve your eruptions or criticisms. You can offer tough feedback with kindness. Kindness allows the other person to trust and hear you.

Remember feedback is about supporting someone to reinforce helpful behavior and change unhelpful behavior to allow them to achieve the expectation. It's not about taking out an opponent who stands between you and your goal.

Two Kinds of Feedback

There are two types of feedback.

The type we are most familiar with, and likely most dread, is redirection feedback. This feedback looks at behavior that is not working or where expectations are not being met and is designed to foster a change in the behavior.

The second type of feedback is reinforcing feedback. It is just as important as redirection feedback and is often overlooked. When someone is meeting the standard or exceeding expectations, reinforcing feedback brings attention to the desired behavior by specifically naming it and encourages continuation and expansion of the exemplary behavior.

Ironically, it is the reinforcing feedback that creates momentum for good to great performance. When an employee knows what the expected performance is and is offered recognition for positive steps to get there, those positive actions expand. Not only that, other employees who are observing where you place your attention pick up the clue and may desire to have some of that sugar sprinkled on them, too. This leads to better behavior choices all around.

The Feedback Formula

Although we want to be natural and conversational with our feedback (remembering direct, factual, neutral, and kind), it helps to have a method to frame the conversation. That's where the feedback formula comes in.

All feedback will be better received if it is preceded by an engaged opening. This creates connection and may help to lower defenses. You must be sincere with the engaged opening. Otherwise you are delivering the traditional crap sandwich where an insincere opening and closing mask poor criticism in the middle.

Beginning with the engaged opening, the formula unfolds in a way that creates authenticity, approachability, trust, and communication.

Engaged Opening

    S – Situation
    B – Behavior
    I – Impact
    C – Change or Continue

Encouraging Closing

Engaged Opening

People will not hear you if they feel threatened – emotionally or physically. Fear limits the ability to listen. Your only job, when opening a feedback conversation, is to make it safe for someone to engage in the conversation. You do that by framing the situation, encouraging listening, and welcoming their comments.

Situation

The transition from the engaged opening sets the stage for exactly what you are going to be talking about. "I would like to talk with you about_____." What situation are you discussing?

Behavior

Focus your feedback on the behavior that was observed in the situation that created the performance issue or unfulfilled expectation. You focus on behavior because it is observable and dynamic and, thus, can be changed through choice or practice. This keeps the feedback from devolving into criticism or personal attacks. This is also true for reinforcing feedback. It's the behavior, not the personality, to which you want to call attention.

Impact

Like the ripple from a stone thrown into a pond, every behavior has a consequence. We call that impact. The behavior choice or action has created a ripple. It's had an impact. Help the person receiving feedback to understand the cause and effect. This ownership creates a desire to change (or continue) the behavior.

Change

If your feedback is redirecting behavior so that performance expectations can be met, something must change. The agreed upon change will bring the other person back into alignment with expectations and outcomes and good performance. The change must be a specific action or set of actions and an agreement is to be made, including any resources that might be needed.

Continue

Feedback for good to great performance is effective when you can congratulate the person and ask that they continue. Create a specific agreement to continue or enhance what is currently being done in order to stay in the range of expected or exemplary performance.

Encouraging Closing

A key job of any leader is to inspire their followers. When you close a feedback conversation with encouragement – real, felt, and genuine – your employee will know that you care and are vested in their success. Offer a word of encouragement, a sincere thank you for the conversation, an assurance of good follow up. This leads the person on the receiving end back into their work with confidence and connection.

From the Client Vault

Frank was a client. He was the visionary and COO of a good-sized family business. He used to bark feedback and rules at people. He used judgement and criticism as a weapon. People were afraid of him and the family relationships were fractured.

He was oblivious to it all.

He also had a high need to be liked.

With that blindspot and the desire for popularity, he was uncomfortable with the vulnerability of offering feedback to another. His discomfort led to pushing his opinions and criticism and people shut down.

When Frank combined his newly acquired listening and open-ended question skills with the SBIC formula, he found a winning combination. Seemingly overnight, he was able to offer improvement, feedback that was motivated by goodwill and delivered with FDNK (factual, direct, neutral and kind). Performance improved, family connection improved, his health improved, and his business skyrocketed.

Managing Your Energy – The 20/60/20 Rule

Who do you spend most of your time with at work? The problem employee or the exemplary employee?

The majority of leaders who are asked this question will admit they spend most of their time with the employee who is the squeaky wheel and underperforms. Why? A myriad of reasons. You've been taught the science of discipline and PIPs (performance improvement plans) and other performance improvement initiatives. You put on your cape and adopt the Hero in you to save the employee, thereby creating a false sense of movement and meaning. The brain is wired to grab onto negatives, so that's the first thing you see every day.

What's the impact?

Pretend that your employees are sitting on a spectrum. On average 10 to 20% will likely fall into the "problem" category and another 10 to 20% into the "high-performing" category. That leaves the middle group in the "OK" to "good" performing category.

This is the 20/60/20 rule.

What percentage of your time are you spending with the bottom performing 20%? You are likely spending 60 to 90% of your precious energy, thought leadership, creativity, and innovation focused on this group.

It gets worse. Less than 10% of energy is focused on the high performers rationalized by, "They don't need it," or "They are already doing a great job," or "I don't have to worry about them." Even the hardiest of plants wither and die without water.

Now, look at the middle group. Engaged in the drama of the attention paid to the underperformers, they have little external encouragement to perform much above the standard expectation.

You must change the focus.

Offer reinforcing feedback to the high performers. Your organization will pay attention to what you pay attention to – creating a road map for high performance. You may hear something like, "It's not fair. You are favoring so and so." Of course you are. You have committed to pay attention to the high performer. Your middling performers will catch on.

In the meantime, you must "contain" the bottom percentage. Not through criticism or punishment. Rather, you create well-stated and non-negotiable performance or behavior standards. You are crystal clear on the expectations, ensuring they have the resources and training to get the job done, and set up a coaching/feedback loop to check in on expectation achievement. Crystal-clear expectations and inspection creates the path for improvement or termination.

With the bottom contained and the top being recognized, the middle is called to a higher performance level and you get some of your energy back.

Why Don't We Do Feedback Well?

You get triggered. When others get defensive, it's natural to become triggered and withdraw into your own defensiveness. The conversation devolves and is not productive. Begin to take the management of your triggers seriously.

You want to rescue. If you do rescue, you take away the accountability and problem solving the other person can offer.

You are uncomfortable with conflict. Be aware of your own discomfort about offering feedback and use some of your strategies to manage your emotions. The other person is on high alert due to their own discomfort and is likely to pick up on yours, causing them to feel unsafe in the conversation. The result may be even more defensiveness.

You are offering the gift of feedback, but you cannot make the other person open your gift. You can, however, take some steps that will make you more effective.

To maintain trust and openness, it's important to say what you see with respect and compassion. If you feel the other person is getting prickly or defensive, kindly bring attention to it. Acknowledge that it is normal to be defensive. Ask what would make it easier for them to receive feedback.

While you're at it, make sure that you are using the SBIC model and focusing on behavioral observation and fact rather than your opinion. Be scrupulous about this.

The impact statement will always be your friend as it makes the feedback meaningful to the person receiving it. This is especially important if the feedback is mission-critical. Make sure the other person understands the impact of the behavior or situation and the potential consequences that may arise if it is left unchanged.

Remember the engaging approach to create emotional safety before launching into any type of feedback. This is an especially important step for managing defensiveness. However, you must make sure you are sincere as the radar is up for any suspected disingenuous behavior.

Be wise. If the situation is only going to be made worse by offering feedback at a given moment, don't do it. Offer it later when emotions have evened out

People want to be liked. Feedback can be interpreted as the opposite – you not liking them. They may take it personally. Just practice. With your continued improvement over time, even the most defensive of people will be more open to your feedback.

Mindset to Improve Your Feedback Skill

As much as there is a discipline to the art of difficult conversation, there's a mindset that precedes it.

Logically, we know that when communication is effective, improvement occurs, knowledge expands, and relationships strengthen.

You might consider yourself an effective communicator and, granted, you likely have natural talent. But natural talent can become stale or even atrophy when left unnurtured.

*Great athletes and musicians and artists, who **practice** their discipline to **improve** their skills, also recognize the power of **mindset.***

Why do you struggle? Let's look at the three mindsets to find out.

1. You lack empathy
   - Being factual and logical are important to having clear communication. When you fail to weave in understanding and empathy for how others think and feel, you may become so focused on the task at hand that you fail to connect.
2. You have been socialized to be polite
   - You have likely been conditioned since childhood to be polite and not to hurt people's feelings. If you feel someone might be hurt, you may withhold important feedback. The truth, told with compassion and neutral fact, will truly set you free (if you are willing to hear it!).
3. You want others to like you, so you are unwilling to rock the boat
   - This is the most self-justified mindset of all. Of course, you want people to like you and regard you well. People sometimes want to blame the messenger. Trust and respect are a more powerful gift than being liked. Be willing to move through discomfort to support others to be the best they can be.

Pay attention to your mindset so that you can be direct, neutral, factual, and kind. You will be able to suspend your judgments and assumptions. You will be authentic and feedback will be offered in the spirit of improvement.

Mindset shifts are like muscle shifts. You don't bench press 250 pounds on your first day of training. You practice until you become better. You celebrate the small wins. You forgive your mistakes. Each day,

- Look for *opportunities* to tell the truth with compassion.
- Find ways to say what you need to say in *fewer words*
- Observe the *emotional feeling* you get from another without needing to soothe it.
- Correct your *mindset setbacks* as soon as you notice them.

With practice, you will create safety for you and for others. This safety is surrounded in trust and respect and provides a space for people to grow.

In Closing – Easy Feedback

You may still wonder if you will hurt someone's feelings. You might still offer your feedback as opinion or assumption rather than fact and behavior. You can rehearse and rehearse, but you may still be confused about what really needs to be said and in what emotional state it will be shared.

Not to worry. When you get out of your head and into your heart, you offer simple, straightforward, and sincere feedback. In the present moment. No rehearsal needed. Simply connect with the other person and neutrally offer observation of factual behavior.

In your heart, you are fully present and ready to offer in the spirit of improvement.

Remember feedback is a gift.

In summary, here are 7 steps to get you ready to deliver improvement-based and useful feedback:

1. **Consider Timing**
   Don't wait too long and don't jump the gun. Give yourself enough space (especially if your emotions are engaged) to consider the behavior as it relates to expectations and outcomes. Remember that too much space will cause the feedback to lose its purpose, however.

2. **Focus on Behavior Rather than Opinion**
   Keep your feedback judgment-free by focusing on the one behavior that, if modified, could do the most to shift performance.

3. **Understand your Emotions**
   We are humans and made up of all kinds of overt and covert emotions. Be aware when you are triggered or judgmental. Get curious with yourself so that you can be clear for the other person.

4. **Get to the Point**

   Don't dance around the issue. Factual and neutral are the preferred ways of being. Neutral is a set point. Make sure to find out what neutral feels like for you.

5. **Identify the Impact**

   Make sure that the person you are offering feedback to understands the impact. We often have a blind eye to the ripples our behaviors can cause. Understanding impact creates a desire to change.

6. **Create an Action Agreement**

   Clarify the request and action steps and then shake hands on the agreement. Ensure that the other person is taking the action steps and that the task does not simply fall back on you. You are there to support.

7. **Laser Focus, Not Razor Focus**

   Laser in on the issue and bring a spotlight to the behavior, impact, and change. Do not use the razor of judgment, assumptions, and opinions to cut to the point.

These seven steps are a great jump-start to aligning head and heart. That alignment is a hallmark of the humanized leader.

With great feedback you create safety for people to learn and course correct. You also create empowerment for achieving goals and positive outcomes.

As you become more skilled at offering feedback, you will begin to see that all of the preceding lessons and skills play a role in delivering great feedback: emotional management, customized communication, great listening, and open-ended questions are all necessary. Your commitment to practicing all of the key mindset and communication skills will make your feedback come across as natural and simple.

Action Steps

1. Scan your environment. Who in your organization needs to receive feedback so that their performance or results see improvement?
2. Use the formula and offer the feedback.
3. Practice a ratio for one week: Offer 3 reinforcing (appreciating) feedback conversations for every single redirecting feedback conversation you deliver.
4. Ask a trusted colleague for feedback on your leadership. Ask, "Am I committed to being the best leader I can possibly be? I would be grateful for any feedback you could offer to me."

PHASE III
PERFORMANCE LEADERSHIP

You may be an expert at managing emotions and you may be an impeccable communicator, but if you are not able to elicit accountability and performance, your leadership abilities will not flourish. Importantly, your team will not elevate into the humanized leaders that they were meant to be.

Phase three is where the rubber meets the road. This is where your expectations are clearly communicated and understood, people are invited into integrity and accountability, and agreements are made that elevate business results.

Warning. This is not easy, but it IS worth it.

9

LEADERSHIP SECRET WEAPON - BUILDING A CULTURE OF ACCOUNTABILITY

"I just can't seem to hold people accountable. I tell them what to do and get the nods and the OK's and then when the time comes for delivery, I get nothing at worst and half at best."

"Why does it feel like I am the only one who cares? I feel like I am the only one pulling any weight around here. It's exhausting."

> "There is no greater fraud than a promise not kept."
>
> – Gaelic Proverb

"Why don't people do what they say they will? It's like pulling teeth to get a project finished these days."

Does this sound familiar?

Why won't people get the work done on time? On budget? As promised? As agreed?

A "lack of accountability" is the stink bomb of our modern society. It's easy to make a dinner date and just as easy to blow it off. We long for the simpler days when a person kept their word.

The pace of the leader is the pace of the pack

You can look outside of yourself for the causes in this lapse of account-ability, yet this book is about your personal leadership. You will have the opportunity in this chapter to look at accountability from many angles and build skill around agreements, expectation setting, and how to deal with the consequences of broken agreements. For now, remember that this is about you improving you.

You have more power and influence than you realize when it comes to creating a culture of accountability, surrounding yourself with accountable people, and living with the personal integrity of being a commitment maker and a promise keeper.

Break out of the "it's happening to me" paradigm and personally choose to make accountability and promise-keeping of the utmost importance. Make every decision and have every conversation from the lens of "what promises am I making or inferring and can I deliver on them?" as well as from the lens of "what commitments am I asking of others and do they have what they need in order to execute the tasks to achieve the desired outcomes?"

The word "accountability" can get a bad rap. Think about the word. Does it evoke positive connotations or mostly negative ones? In many ways, accountability has devolved into the consummate "gotcha." "I am going to hold you accountable" contains the inner dialogue and implicit understanding of "When things go wrong, I am going to blame you." No wonder that many are reluctant to raise their hands and say, "I will be accountable." For many, it's better to hide and hope for the best.

> "Many people have come to believe that an adequate explanation can excuse a poor result."
>
> – Anonymous

You know that you have lapses in accountability when you are experiencing:

- Missed deadlines
- Putting a spin on bad news
- Passivity in meetings – nodding yet not committing
- Gossip
- Venting behind closed doors

What if you were deeply committed to leading from a place of accountability? What if you became a person of your word? What if you clearly communicated expectations? What if you developed an inspection process that didn't resemble micro-managing? What if you asked curious questions to deduce why projects were not completed, why quality was amiss, why mile markers were not met? What if you taught your team to do the same while asking, "What's best for the customer/company/team? What if you did not back down from another's defensiveness and lovingly held your ground? You would have a culture of accountability. You would be heads above all others in your industry while they still struggle with employees who hide their hands behind their backs when asked to raise them in promise.

Let's take the stink off the word and explore its simplest definitions, as well as the concepts that are accountability's kissing cousins.

Returning to the mothership of words, the Merriam-Webster dictionary, the definition of accountable is:

1. Subject to giving an account; being answerable
2. Capable of being explained; being explainable

When one promises to be accountable, they promise to give an accurate account, which means that they are answerable to effort and outcome. The effort and outcome can also be explained.

The dictionary definition is not completely satisfying as it relates to accountability in the workplace. That's why several other words are rolled into this overarching concept of accountability.

Let's pull in the cousins.

Commitment *(n.)*:

1. an agreement or pledge to do something in the future — a *commitment* to improve conditions at the prison
2. something pledged — the *commitment* of troops to the war
3. the state or an instance of being obligated or emotionally impelled — a *commitment* to a cause

Promise *(n.)*:

1. a declaration that one will do or refrain from doing something specified
2. a legally binding declaration that gives the person to whom it is made a right to expect or to claim the performance or forbearance of a specified act
3. reason to expect something; little *promise* of relief
4. ground for expectation of success, improvement, or excellence; shows considerable *promise*

What we are really talking about is a full and meaningful word – Integrity:

1. firm <u>adherence</u> to a code of especially moral or artistic values : incorruptibility
2. an unimpaired condition : soundness
3. the quality or state of being complete or undivided : completeness

Trust me, you will not be satisfied with somebody simply adding up and presenting their list of tasks and actions. Wrapped into the desires to have accountability, accountable teams and a culture of accountability are the concepts of commitment and promise. You can see that it all leads to integrity.

Look at the mechanics. The company sets an outcome, which can be accounted for and explained. The action begins when you ask for commitment and promises are made to achieve the outcome. Then, the actions are taken and outcome is achieved. You now operate with integrity.

This makes accountability a mouthful, yes?

Can you, then, "hold someone accountable"? Yes. Only in the way of obtaining a measure and an explanation. If you want a team to be accountable, you must create a culture that values measurement and explanation and wrap it in the practice of making clear commitments, keeping promises, and acting with impeccable integrity.

Create an environment where they choose to participate, complete agreements, and opt for accountability. They must be willing to account for their actions, explain the process and results, make a commitment, and keep a promise. You, as the leader, can be a huge influence in other people's choice to be accountable. Walk your talk.

This starts with you, the leader. Take a moment now to take stock. Where are you weak or strong? What is one thing you can do to become a more integrous leader?

To sum it up:

Accountability is the act of factually and neutrally taking account of assumptions, judgements, criticisms, or emotions. You have things to look at and things to count, and can attribute a degree of responsibility or action to each of them. Once this initial activity is completed, you seal the deal with a commitment and a promise.

The Three Aspects to Creating a Culture of Accountability

There are three aspects to creating a culture of accountability:

One - setting appropriate expectations
Two - taking 100% responsibility
Three - creating intentional agreements

Expectation setting always comes first. When people understand exactly what they have agreed to by understanding both the desired outcome and sub-outcomes (actions), they stand a greater chance of taking responsibility and being accountable to any agreements made.

It can be as simple as that.

The difference between accountability and responsibility is that responsibility is shared, and accountability is agreed to by individuals – either by you or the other members of the team. You are answerable to your actions and accountability is measured once the actions have been taken and outcome evaluated. Responsibility is ongoing commitment and is shared among those who have agreed to the outcome or actions. This adds flavor to any agreement and robust commitment in a culture of accountability. Good!

When you add intentional agreements, which is the formula that makes accountability actionable, you have a path to a culture of accountability.

"Great leaders understand that talented people thrive in a culture where accountability is a support system for success."

– Daniel Pink

From the Beginning: Expectations

A culture of accountability requires that you first start by communicating what success looks like. Your job is to set crystal-clear expectations and then role model the behaviors associated with that expectation. People cannot agree to that which they are not clear about. Yet, they do it all the time. This is what creates the frustration born out of lack of accountability. If you don't establish your desired outcome, you will get what you get.

This simple step of setting clear and actionable expectations is easily overlooked. Perhaps you are moving swiftly and don't communicate fully. You try to be expedient or maybe you assume that they "should know what to do." Yet, setting expectations is the quickest way to getting what you want. Expectations are the outcomes required to obtain the goal, live within the cultural norms, uphold the values, do the job well. Often, they are implicit. It's time to get them out in the open.

Step One: Set Them

Tell people what the successful outcome looks like. Show them the desired result based upon the vision you are communicating. Don't stop there. Make sure that they get it. Can they repeat back to you the expectation? Do they understand what steps might be needed to create success? Do they have the necessary resources to get the job done? Are they clear about the check-in and inspection process? Have they agreed to the outcome?

Communication is a two-way street. In this instance, you must maintain a dialogue during expectation setting. Like the carpenter measuring twice prior to cutting, let your crystal-clear communication do the work for you. Here are some suggestions to improve your two-way communication: Introduce the bulleted list that follows.

- Communicate what success looks like (onboarding, new job assignment, department goal, the vision).
- Probe for understanding. Does your team member fully understand the expectation? If not, clarify your communication.
- If there are specific milestones that must be met, communicate those as well as any pertinent timelines.
- Be curious and ask your team member how they think they might go about achieving the expectation. This gives you an opportunity to understand how they think.
- Ask questions. Brainstorm possible steps. Be willing to see the execution from their lens, rather than your prescription.
- Offer resources.
- Offer encouragement and the belief that the expectation will be executed well.
- Schedule appropriate check-ins or set agreed upon guidelines for checking progress.

Step Two: Check In

Once you have set the expectation, you must check in on progress. Do this in a way that is respectful. You want to bump them back to the expectation if they have gone in a wayward direction. You want to encourage them while assuring that things are on track. Do this in a way that is not satisfying some need in you to micro-manage, dictate the how-to's, or criticize the process.

Consider this scenario:

It is May 1st. Your team of 10 is asked to take a solo trip from New York to San Francisco. That means there are ten different solo trips, each finding their way to San Francisco. Each team member has a budget of $5,000.

The expectation is that each person is to arrive in San Francisco no later than June 15th and must arrive with a portion of the allocated budget, at least $100.00. That's it – 10 trips each with a budget of $5,000 to arrive in San Francisco by June 15th with a surplus of at least $100.00. The expectation is clarified and is clearly understood.

You now have a clarified, unified expectation that will be delivered in ten different ways. Perhaps someone drives a car and takes the southern route and enjoys the Grand Canyon along the way. Another goes north and brings back tales of Moab Utah and the incredible crags and rocks. Still, another drives straight through to San Francisco to explore the remarkable city.

Interesting.

Each has arrived in San Francisco on time with the required surplus of budget, as expected. Yet, in each of their adventures, you have learned new and different methods to get to the destination. You can debrief to find out which was the best, added the most value, was most efficient, was most fun. Now apply this to any work situation where a diversity of experience and answers would add value to your strategy.

The team can help you identify the steps of your crystal-clear expectation. This is when team accountability ratchets up for your organization. How can you take this simple scenario and apply it to your business as you are building a culture of accountability?

Step Three: Follow Up

Inspect what you expect. An expectation has been set, milestones agreed to, and check-in time is here. Review the original expectations against the achievement and offer feedback or recognition. Debrief the original under-standing and the execution. Adjust for next time. Evaluate team performance. Evaluate your original communication. Be neutral and thorough.

This simple act of inspection defines how serious you are about accountability. If you communicated it, you meant it. If they accepted it, they agreed. If you inspect and debrief it, it takes on additional importance. Involve all concerned in the debriefing process. If you debrief from a place of learning, with neutrality and curiosity, you will be better able to surface most of the hidden issues.

To sum it up, you cannot make great agreements on something you have no detail about. You can't take responsibility for executing on agreements when you navigate in the unknown. Use expectations like a religion. As a matter of fact, teach your team how to brainstorm and set expectations for themselves. You will then have a team of problem-solving goal setters. Magic!

Accepting 100% Responsibility

Sue Paige, who founded personal development firm Pathways to Successful Living, teaches a concept called "Intentions Equal Results." At first it is a mind boggler. If you have a crappy marriage, you are likely to defend to the ends of the world that it was never your intention to have a crappy marriage. Yet, there you are…in an unhappy situation, a dead-end relationship, filled with what-ifs and blame. You say you never intended it and your results tell a different story.

> "Intentions equal results"
> – Sue Paige, founder of Pathways to Successful Living

Where is the gap where self-sabotage occurs?

- What you say you want and what you get
- What commitments you make and what you do

What if you took 100% responsibility for your outcomes? What if you truly came to embrace the wisdom of "intentions equal results?" If your intention was to have a wonderful and loving marriage, you would be making different choices, promises, and commitments. You would be having conversations you might normally avoid. You would be communicating your expectations and sharing what success looks like. You would be listening in a way that might surprise you. You would be doing different things to get a better result.

This is true for every area of your life and business. 100% responsibility means just that. I have what I have based upon the choices I made or I didn't make. I hear the argument already – "I talk and talk until I'm blue in the face and I still can't get my team to commit and be accountable." Stop talking and begin acting. What are the consequences for lack of accountability? What is the inspiration for it? How do you create a culture where the TEAM holds each other accountable?

Here are some great ideas to get into the 100% responsibility game:

- Stop blaming others and ask questions to learn the root cause of the issue
- Role model what you expect from others
- Find out what your contribution was if there is a lapse in accountability
- Debrief with others and inquire how the situation could be different
- Retrace your contribution steps to the positive outcome

Just a little word to the wise: If someone doesn't keep a commitment with you, they are 100% responsible the first time. By the third time, you are completely responsible for producing that result in your life.

If you understand this, it will change your paradigm around accountability. 100% responsibility implies that whoever is making the agreement, whether it be two people or ten people, each person in that agreement has 100% responsibility for the outcome. If two people are involved, that means 200% responsibility (twice the effort) and if ten are involved, you have 1000% responsibility. If each person said I have 100% responsibility, think of what support and action and effort and accountability would look like.

What usually happens is that you make an agreement with another and "split up" the responsibility in accordance to the split in actions.

For example, let's factor that 50% of the work goes to you and that 50% of the work goes to me. If we operate from this 50/50 mindset, we pay attention to our own task and don't have much investment in supporting the other to meet their 50%.

When I get the entire 50% of my tasks done then I have a false sense of winning, but I don't win at all if you've only done 20%. We agreed to the outcome – together – and now we're going to blow past the deadline and fail to keep our agreement.

100% responsibility says that whatever we agree to, we have both feet in and we're equally responsible for the outcome. This means that I'm checking on you and supporting you and you are doing the same for me. The result is we get across the finish line together.

What this doesn't mean is that I take on your work or become a victim of your actions.

This will change everything for you if you get this and you begin to practice this and ask for this from other people.

> *"Accountability breeds response-ability."*
>
> – Stephen R. Covey

Make Intentional Agreements

Remember responsibility is the ability to respond.

With that in mind, agreements become the mechanics we choose to fulfill, or that which we have counted and understood as important for accountability. Agreements are the system employed in order to be 100% responsible for what we have said we are going to do.

The combination of 100% responsibility and the steps of creating agreements establishes a solid platform for integrity which leads to inescapable accountability.

When you understand and see the facts (outcomes/expectations), you can agree and assume responsibility for action.

A great agreement, supported by a crystal-clear expectation, is the greatest tool you have in creating a culture of accountability. Solid agreements are the foundation for trust.

What are the components of an agreement?

- Both parties agree
- Both parties win

- Together you create something more than could be created individually
- Commitment to the outcome is assured
- Both parties take 100% responsibility for the outcome and support each other to keep the commitment

Take a moment for self-reflection. What does 100% responsibility mean to you as you make an agreement with another person?

The best agreements are made in SMART format. You will remember that as:

Specific

Measurable

Action-based

Realistic

Time-bound

Broken Agreements

How do you feel when someone breaks an agreement with you? What's the impact on trust? How likely are you to make another agreement with that person willingly and freely?

Broken agreements erode trust. When someone breaks an agreement, you can either go into your protection shell, not say a word, and guard your heart. Or...you can bring the broken agreement into the conversation and inquire about it. What happened? What were your intentions when you first made the agreement? What changed? How can I support you to get back into agreement, if that is something you want? Discuss the impact on the relationship and future agreements. Then, either renegotiate or agree to abandon the agreement.

You may want to do a quick debrief with only yourself. What about the agreement may have been unclear or loosely defined? How might there have been indications that the other person did not fully agree? How did you ask for commitment at the close of the agreement-making?

Renegotiating or Counteroffers

If it appears that you will either break the agreement or that something has changed which impacts the ability of the agreement to be fulfilled, you can renegotiate. When do you renegotiate? BEFORE the agreement is broken. Many miss this option for fear of upsetting the apple cart or disappointing others. They remain stuck in wishful thinking, hoping that the gods will appear with a solution. They fail to address the impending broken agreement until far too late.

Reach out to the other party and explain the situation and ask for a renegotiation. Nine times out of ten, you will get it. Or…if you truly cannot or don't want to complete the agreement, be honest about that. Things change all the time and the agreements we make in good faith may become null and void prior to completion. Be honest. Be timely.

What if you are asked to create an agreement and parts (or all) of it don't work for you? Make a counteroffer. "This I can do. This part I cannot. What I'm willing to do instead is this." You'd be better off having this conversation than committing to something you don't fully agree with and then breaking the agreement later. Agreements must be win/win for them to work.

Just Say "No"

Why do you make agreements that you have no intention of keeping? Why do you make agreements that don't fit into your life? Into your calendar? Into your interests? You likely make them to be socially polite, to not rock the boat, so that people will like you. Be honest and be real. If the agreement states a Tuesday night networking and Tuesday night is already date night on your calendar, just say no.

Your personal integrity is at stake. Again, just say no – no, thank you.

Agreements with Self

There is nobody more important than you and nothing more important than the agreements you keep with yourself. If you were honest, you'd admit you are usually the first person with whom you break an agreement. The impact on trusting yourself and your personal integrity is crushing when this is a regular habit.

All Leaders Inspired clients go through an eye-opening exercise at this juncture in our group work. Called "Broken Agreements with Self," it is loosely borrowed from an old article (the author of which I wish we could credit...) that described a year-end evaluation process. Take 20 to 60 minutes right now and complete this. Be prepared to uncover some major self-knowledge.

Broken Agreements with Self Exercise

Part One:
1. Take out a sheet of paper.
2. Draw three circles.
3. Inside each of the circles, write three major life goals you have and are important to you. (i.e. buy a house, a fully-funded retirement account, get a master's degree, etc.)
4. Take a moment to visualize the achievement of each of these goals, paying attention to the emotion that comes up.

Part Two:
1. For each of the goal circles, consider the promises and agreements you've made with yourself that you have broken and arrange them around each of the relevant circles (i.e. A weight loss goal might have broken agreements such as, "ate the fast food," "hit snooze and missed the gym," "ordered pizza instead of preparing the salad," "walked ¼ mile instead of the mile").
2. Take your time with this and do this until you feel complete for each circle.
3. Take a moment to assess how you feel about what you've discovered.

Part Three:
1. Choose an action to take for each of the circles (you will have 3 actions) that you will write down as a SMART agreement with yourself and take those actions immediately to create momentum.

For a short video and pdf download of this exercise, visit www. thehumanizedleader.com/bonus

A Word of Encouragement

A young man who was in one of the first sessions where this exercise was used took his contemplation to heart. He realized that he wanted to live closer to his family, own a house, and be in a loving relationship. Within a year, he found employment in the town next to his family, closed on a house, and reconnected with his high school sweetheart and was deeply in love. It can happen!

As you keep agreements with yourself, you will stand inside integrity and it will make it a thousand times easier to keep agreements with other people.

Shadow Accountability

An odd and implicit agreement we make and keep with others is revealed in the concept of "shadow accountability."

Where in your life do you have a wink and a nod with another person when it comes to making and keeping agreements? Where do you have an implicit agreement that says, "If I don't call you on your behavior, you won't call me on mine"? How often do you find yourself not asking others to be accountable knowing that out of politeness or agreement, they are bound to let you slip out of your promises?

This is not conscious! Your ego has convinced you that you have a good thing going on here. What you really have is a big shadow where there is the appearance of activity. This is nothing but a shadow agreement in which the talk is enough, no action is needed, and you will never mention it to each other again.

Let's look at a typical process: If I ask you to be accountable to an agreement, I must be accountable also. I may not want to be pinned down. So, if I don't pin you down, perhaps you won't pin me down either. If I'm loose with deadlines, success metrics, and ironclad agreements, then you can be loose with me also.

Shadow Accountability is a form of collusion that keeps us safe, just in case things don't work out. When we are in the shadow things don't get done, integrity is damaged, resistance ensues, and we all go around and around in the same spiral.

Wow! What a setup.

You've learned through this chapter that accountability is defined as the quality of being answerable to another for actions taken. You can answer to yourself or can answer to another individual or group. At the core of it, a promise is made: You agree to answer for an action you have agreed to take.

If you shy away from direct, neutral and fact-based discussions, you may find it hard to ask for accountability or deliver the bad news when others don't keep up their end of the deal.

Accountability is impossible if you are worried about hurting someone's feelings or committed to enabling others.

It can be elusive when you make agreements that, unconsciously or habitually, you don't intend to keep.

A Very Special Shadow – The Back Door

When you live in the shadow, you have a back door to every agreement you make.

This crack in the door shows up as the excuses you make – real or imagined – that justify (in your mind) why you could not meet the agreement you made.

Even a sliver of an opening around your noble reasons, the kid's needs, your boss's demands gives you a way to slip out the back. Making another thing more important without renegotiating the first agreement creates that trusty escape hatch.

Be aware of where you're tolerating your excuses around agreements or justifying your reasons for not executing them.

That's your back door. And you've got to shut those back doors firmly.

The Path to Success

There is a way out of this shadow. Some we have already discussed in this chapter bear repeating.

Create criteria for yourself so that you understand when to say yes, or no, to an agreement. When you make agreements you intend to keep, you have more invested in the outcome.

When you make the agreement, remember that it's not a 50/50 or 60/40 split. Rather you assume 100% responsibility for the outcome. And the other person must commit 100% as well. That's 200% effort towards achieving the agreement.

Ask specific questions to make a solid agreement. Start with the 5 W's (who, what, when, where, and why). Loosely stated agreements can fall apart quickly. Success can be achieved more quickly when all parties are clear about the steps and outcome.

Check in on progress. Not to be confused with micromanagement, checking in means offering consistent support, creating collaboration opportunities, becoming a brainstorming partner, or simply offering encouragement.

Don't dictate the terms of the agreement. People are more ener- gized and committed when they feel they have ownership and control. Let all parties name and claim their action steps. Then, make sure to acknowledge success.

We have all been let down and we have all missed deadlines. We have also all been at the mercy of mandated timelines. How have your experiences of accountability impacted your actions and attitudes or the actions and attitudes of others? Can you recognize when the shadow appears, and the back door of excuses opens?

The next time you are making an agreement and want to hold yourself or others accountable, reread this section and practice some of the tools.

When you continue to shed light on the shadow, make agreements you intend to keep and allow yourself to be specific. Your leadership will shine.

The Culture of Accountability Starts with You

All roads lead back to the leader – to you! Your team will model the behavior they observe in you. If you preach accountability and live it at the same time, it will be seen as important and desirable. If you have an accountability slip-up and publicly admit it, accountability will be seen as important and desirable. If you debrief, check in, and inspect on a regular basis, accountability will be seen as important and desirable.

The only way is through. Be impeccable with your word and scrupulous with your actions.

Action Steps

1. Contemplate and journal about:
2. The last time someone broke an agreement with you. How did you stay in the responsibility game?
3. Someone interrupting you the first time. Someone interrupting you for the third time. How do you stay in the responsibility game?
4. How does the belief that problems come from "out there" keep you out of accountability?
5. Take stock of your current agreements and...
6. Decide which are solid agreements you intend to keep.
7. Decide which agreements you know you will not keep and take the steps to renegotiate or say no.
8. Decide which agreements in your life are either very loose or unspoken and tighten them.

10

LEADERS TELL THE TRUTH

Lie is a charged word. Feel your body as you read, "You are likely a liar." Where do you feel the push against? In your stomach? In your throat? Do you flush? This is a big trigger word. Lie. Liar. It brings forth years and years of childhood shame over fibbing, spinning, withholding, or outright whoppers.

This chapter is going to challenge you and tick you off at the same time. Stick with it. As you observe your own relationship with the truth, from the scientist's perspective of neutrality, you will see what you can do to live as a fuller and more authentic communicator. Promise!

As a way of introduction, let's look at the societal "secret nod" to lying. Believe me, this is not your fault.

Can you remember what you were told as a child about telling the truth? Maybe this sounds familiar:

"You should always tell Mommy/Daddy/Teacher the truth."

"It's a sin to lie."

"You can tell Mommy anything."

"If you lie, you will be in big trouble."

"If you are not telling me the truth right now, you will be punished."

"You lied to me? I'm so disappointed in you."

"You better be good and tell the truth. Santa Claus is watching…"

Add your own here: _____

This is a set-up. Let's have a reality check. Meet Billy Brown and his mom, Mrs. Brown. Billy is a good boy and he has been taught right and wrong by his mom and dad. Billy wants to be a good boy and he always wants to tell the truth because that's what Mom has taught him.

Cue Camera:

(Billy and Mrs. Brown walk through Target and they spy their neighbor, Mrs. Culliver, who lives down the street. They approach each other.)

Billy: "Hi Mrs. Culliver." (waving and within earshot)

Billy: "Mommy, why is Mrs. Culliver so fat?"

Mrs. Brown: "Billy!! Shhhh. Don't say that. It's rude and it hurts Mrs. Culliver's feelings."

Billy: (confused...)

Mrs. Culliver: (looking sad)

Mrs. Brown: "I'm so sorry, Jean. Sometimes the oddest things just pop out of his mouth."

Billy: (feeling shame and looks at his feet)

I am certain that something similar has happened in your life. Or maybe you've experienced it with your children or younger family members. In that moment, what was Bobby taught? Right! It is not safe to say what is truthful for you. When you say the truth out loud, you could be punished. Even if Mommy says you should always tell the truth.

Humans are conditioned to lie to protect societal norms. If you simply blurted every "truth" that popped into your head, that would be troubling. That "truth" might really be a judgment, or a comparison constructed by your ego and not truthful at all. For little kids, it creates confusion. As you grow older, teenagers at some point (or for some, many points) in their life will lie as they seek to express their independence and autonomy. Into adulthood, you choose to protect your personality, status, or position and it becomes more and more attractive to express half-truths or withhold (another form of lying) in order to keep up and get ahead.

Now, let's add Santa Claus, Disney, and the tooth fairy to the mix…oy!

In case this sounds sanctimonious, know it was written with clear intent. There is a protective thing that happens for all humans that may cause people to be less than truthful at points in their life.

This chapter is going to help get you closer to the truth in your life and your business, supporting your integrity along the way.

The Many Ways People Lie

People avoid telling the truth in the sneakiest of ways, advocating loudly for their point of view.

Take advertising, for instance. This is the perfect avenue for half-truths, spins, and outright lies. How many descriptions of high fructose corn syrup are there, anyway? Why do you have to buy those boots to be cool? Why do you have to be hot and sexy at 50?

People lie to protect their personalities, wanting others to see them in a certain way. Think of those fish tales.

"Early to bed and early to rise Fish like hell and make up lies"

– Anonymous

Lying takes on many forms – some pleasant and others just down-right wrong.

- Spinning a tale
- Withholding
- Whoppers
- The lie that supports the first lie
- Little white lies
- You can add your flavor of lies, half-truths and withholds here…

Why Do Humans Lie?

The list of why is exhaustive because the practice is so pervasive. Generally, you will hear things like, "I was afraid of hurting them." Or someone might say, "If I told them the full truth, they would lose their faith or trust in me." Or maybe you find yourself uttering the immortal words of Jack Nicholson in *A Few Good Men,* "You can't handle the truth."

That last one is particularly interesting. Let's pull it apart. "You can't handle the truth." Really? Who says so? This is a noble statement on the outside, but inside it comes from a desire to control the situation, the perception, and the outcome. Why not give people the option to handle the truth? If you are doing your job of leading the conversation, rather than trying to control the outcome, you will get a lot closer to supporting people to know and understand the truth. Don't validate your own disdain for the tough conversation by putting your discomfort onto someone else and withholding.

At the end of the day, as mentioned earlier in the chapter, we don't tell the full truth (or the truth at all) because we are trying to protect something about our personalities. Let go of that protection mechanism and you are on your path to the kind of open and trusting relationships that will make your life and your business soar.

What's the Impact?

Like a blinding glimpse of the obvious, the impact is trust. You may not overtly feel this, yet you intuitively know when not to trust another person. You know when you are not being told the truth or only being told a partial truth. You are wired to notice this.

However, you've become conditioned to it. It's like that piece of paper on the floor that you've turned a blind eye to and neglect to pick up. It's a toleration.

The impact is trust. Let's say it again…THE IMPACT IS TRUST. How can you lead in the way you desire when trust has eroded or been corrupted?

Your success in navigating and managing change, innovation, and growth is directly tied to your willingness to tell the truth. Your employees cry out for transparency, for honest and open conversations. They can sniff out a spin or a withhold or a lie in a minute.

Let's find a way out of this mess that's been created…one step at a time.

The Road Back to the Truth

Here are five effective actions you can take to create the space for more truth in your life and business: The Redo, Own Your Side, Think Before, Trust and Depersonalize, and Question Your Assumptions. Let's look at each.

1.   The Redo

You may remember this from our work around the Drama Triangle. If you find yourself fudging the truth, out yourself immediately. Sales and marketing know that the relationship is almost always enhanced with a customer when a mistake is immediately owned, and steps are taken to make the customer whole. The relationship is elevated in the perfect recovery.

The same is true for missteps in truth. You will be appreciated for acknowledging the truth slip in the moment and for taking responsibility for getting back into truth. First, people feel when something is off, even if they are too polite to say anything about it. When you own it, they are validated. Second, people want to be helpful (and forgiving is helpful). If you sincerely acknowledge that you weren't fully truthful and would like to make it right, people hold you with more esteem. People will want to trust you more. Funny, huh?

Here is a little script that might help:

- "I would like to redo this conversation."
- "I wasn't fully honest with you."
- "This is why" ("I was afraid," "I wanted you to like me," "I was protecting my image," etc.)

- "I apologize."
- "This is what is really going on..."
- "I do hope you can forgive me, and I make a pledge to do my best to be nothing but truthful in the future with you."

Can you imagine being on the other end of that humble and truthful conversation? The road back to trust has begun.

2. Own Your Side of the Street – Clear the Air

Clearing up with another person is about owning your side of the street for whatever drama or story you have been carrying around. It's about taking responsibility for your own life and experiences.

When you've carried resentment or judgment, the facts are blurred, and the story takes on a life of its own, creating energetic drag that leads to resistance. Everything becomes more difficult, and when your energy is drained you cannot lead effectively.

What's more, if you don't clear things up, you run the risk of carrying the resentment or bad feelings into a new situation. You become a prisoner to your own story. It's so much easier to deal with the facts while honoring the feeling.

Consider the story of Claire.

Claire was a rising executive in her organization. She was a key confidante of the CEO and regularly was called upon for participation in key meetings and strategic sessions. She was an invaluable executive in the company.

There was only one problem. Even though she led a key division in the organization, she was regularly left out of opportunities to "be at the table."

This came to a head when all executives except Claire were invited to a year-end celebration. Her familiar reaction was to feel victimized and to place blame outside of herself. This led to hard feelings which impacted her willingness – even her ability – to participate.

Thanks to some great coaching, she was able to turn it around and take responsibility for the exclusions. She got curious and asked herself, "What am I doing that creates this outcome?" With that perspective and without blame, she cleared the air with her CEO. She expressed her feelings of disappointment in the exclusions and owned how she had never challenged or asked for inclusion.

This turned out well and illuminated something about which the senior executives were not aware. Claire was included at the highest level from that day forward.

She took responsibility for her situation and had the courage to own her part in it…and the temerity to ask for something different.

Now put yourself in Claire's shoes. Even though her story is not yours, I suspect there is some grievance you've been hanging onto that could be cleared with an open and honest conversation and enable you to create more personal freedom.

The Freedom Formula for Clearing the Air

1. When something happens, acknowledge the facts about it and not the made-up story.
2. Ask yourself, "What is my contribution to this situation?"
3. Unravel the story that you have made up about the situation, including the assumptions about the other person's motive or anything that would cause you to blame your circumstances or feel victimized. This gets you to neutral.
4. Talk to the other person (if not feasible, write it in a letter you will not send). This step is about the facts of the situation, stated without blame, coupled with whatever you need to apologize for and whatever contribution you own.
5. The final step is to move forward – offering what you can to clear this up with specific and clear actions or requests.

For a pdf download of either of the freedom formulas, log onto www.thehumanizedleader.com/bonus

This might seem counterintuitive. Humans are wired to protect their ego. That protection often comes at the price of freedom. Maybe the relationship won't be restored in Step Five, but what is restored is your energy and your integrity and your peace of mind.

If you are aware of this and make clearing the air a regular practice, wonderful things will happen for you, not the least of which is:

- You will release situations that you used to hang on to for years and that drain your energy.
- You will become adept at factually sharing your withheld thoughts and learn to trust what you see and feel.
- You will resolve conflicts swiftly and professionally.
- You will have peace of mind.

A key tenet to Leadership Mastery is knowing that whatever gets created out there is the direct result of something I've done or failed to do. It's not somebody else's fault; I create my own reality.

3.   Thinking Before You Speak or Write

Have you ever been coached to save emails to your drafts folder before sending them? Especially in tense situations where you may not have access to the truth because you are slave to your anger-induced opinion?

Remember the lessons on triggers. Sometimes when triggered, you instinctively blurt out a truth without regard for kindness or appropriateness. Other times you are triggered into full-armored protection and you couldn't find the truth if your life depended upon it.

When you are reacting, you are not thinking anymore. Your sense of reason has been hijacked by emotion. Be aware. You've already developed strategies to lessen the trigger. In this case, time is your friend.

Stop and think. Breathe and think. Take a walk and think. Think about your desired outcome and what's in the best interest for all. With that in mind and with all your thinking centered in your leadership, you are ready to speak or write your response.

4.   Trusting the Other and Depersonalizing the Situation

In other words, question the thought, "They can't handle the truth." They *can* handle the truth if you deliver it with compassion, kindness, and in the spirit of wanting to create a better situation. Your team is more resilient than you give them credit for, and they are crying out for transparency. Withholding the truth with the noble reason of "they can't handle it" is you saying, "I want to control the situation or the narrative." Understand your motives and you will get closer to the truth every time.

And while you are at it, don't take things so personally. Being offended or outraged is the Victim's game. Don't get trapped there. People can be clunky in their communication. The leader has the vision to interpret things in a better light. You cannot do that if you personalize every piece of ill-communicated information or if you decide to own another's criticism.

When someone criticizes, one of two things are true: either 1) It's about them, or 2) They have discovered a problem that needs resolution. Get curious about them and curious about root cause and solution, and you won't have the opportunity to take offense.

5. Questioning the Stories and Assumptions

Remember the road out of drama is found in reflective listening – listening for both emotion and fact. The emotions can lead to stories and assumptions. The facts are your friends.

Be mindful of the things you tell yourself and practice personal inquiry. Is it true? Are you certain? What is fact and what is opinion or judgement? You will often find out that you have told a story to yourself repeatedly until you believe it to be true. It creates a disconnect with your wise self, the part of you that knows the truth. Dig for the facts, question the opinion, own the emotion. What have you assumed to be so?

As you relentlessly practice this for yourself, you can support the others around you to do the same. Listen for fact and feeling. Probe for truth. Do a root cause analysis of where the story started. Help other people to unwind the opinion, judgment, and certainty so they can see the truth. It really does set you free.

Truth Guidelines

You do not have permission to spout truth without some guidelines. Here is your barometer. Follow it ruthlessly, if you want to create communication and trust in your team.

- Is it kind?
- Is it necessary?
- Does it have to be said right now and by you?
- Is it your opinion or fact?

When considering the last question, you must look at the price of assumptions – your opinions. When you make assumptions about situations or people or things, it is perceived through your own filter and you will spin things to your point of view. This creates a system of lies, and it puts you in prison. You are in prison with a great number of other people struggling with their own emotional intelligence. Get out of there – fast!

Truthful Leaders are Humble

Humility is an attractive and necessary characteristic of an emotionally intelligent leader. It's very humbling to become a truth-teller. It's very humbling to do a redo or clear the air with someone. Just take a deep breath and be humbled. It's powerful and it's a great model of behavior for those around you. Bust through the drama of lies and spins and half-truths. Ditch the drama in your work and personal life and make it super easy for yourself:

- Have the conversations you need to have.
- Be compassionate in your communication.
- Tell the best version of the truth that you can in any situation.
- Sniff out drama and bring the light of reality to it.
- Out yourself the minute you slip up, ask for forgiveness and practice a redo.

Here's what you'll get in return:

- You release situations that you used to hang on to for years and years which require you to clean up your side of the street.
- You create situations and relationships based in authenticity and give up any need for the idea that you must lie to preserve yourself.
- Rather than withholding thoughts, you'll share your ideas more factually, trusting other people.
- You trust yourself to share those thoughts that you're holding back.
- You become aware more swiftly of built-up tension and unresolved conflict and have the skills to get to the heart of the conversation and create harmony and action.

Be the leader of your life and be the leader of your business and use this drama-busting to get to those conflicts that need to be resolved because they're distracting to people. Speaking the truth, without blame, will restore connection and trust.

A Word About Performance Appraisals as it Relates to Truth-telling

No discussion about truth-telling would be complete without a word about an often missed opportunity in corporate life. Today's performance appraisal process (rooted in big management practices from the command and control style of the 1960s) does not function as a constant drip of transparent and truthful conversation. Instead it becomes a burdensome and disenfranchising way of creating distrust, protection, and withholding as employees become subject to an often one-sided "evaluation" of a snapshot in time.

Here's what your employees are thinking:

- According to a survey by Trinet and Wakefield, 22 percent of millennials would rather call in sick than face a traditional job performance review. This reflects the pervasive feeling that job reviews are a "trial" where your performance is criticized – rather than an opportunity for personal growth.

- Research by TruQu shows that at least 76% of employees would like to have feedback discussions at least 12 times a year.
- According to a CEB study, 9 out of 10 HR managers don't believe their performance review process is truly accurate. This is partly due to the traditional "rater" and "ratee" system.
- When feedback is delivered from one manager to a single employee, biases and personal feelings taint the data; this makes it less accurate, useful, and actionable.
- From the same study, it was revealed that 47 percent of millennials have started looking for another job after receiving performance review results. The one-off conversation diminishes any trust that they are receiving professional development tools or that their performance is appreciated.
- A 2010 study by the Corporate Executive Board found that companies that encouraged honest feedback and open communication among their staff delivered a 10-year total shareholder return that was 270 percent greater than in other companies – 7.9 percent compared to 2.1 percent.
- According to a survey by the firm Fierce Inc., being polite, politically correct, or sensitive to other people's feelings shouldn't be an organizational priority. The diagnosis revealed a disturbing statistic: 37 percent of respondents felt their organizations suffered from the malady of "terminal niceness," valuing politeness over the pursuit of the best ideas and perspectives.

Let's cut to the chase. Whether you are a performance appraisal lover or hater, what really counts is that you are truthful and transparent in your conversations with others and that those conversations happen frequently. Not only that, you encourage others to be truthful about their concerns, ideas, and dreams by listening and asking great questions – often! Your listening to talking ratio is 80/20. Remember? Let them talk 80% of the time.

Leaders Inspired has encouraged clients to adopt the Talent Conversation Model. This moves the conversation from a 1 to 5 formal ranking system to a series of truthful and open conversations about career path and talent development. These conversations are empowering to both parties and a great way to be clear about success measures, expectations, and current/future performance.

In Closing

Be a truth-seeker and a truth-teller and teach others to do the same by example all day long. This is your integrity. This is your role modeling. This is your path to creating long-lasting, impactful, and wonderfully engaging relationships with your team. This is the secret key to emotional intelligence. Use the key to open the door to your freedom.

Action Steps

1. Use the formula to clear the air of any resentment or unresolved situation.
2. Use the truth formula to instantly own any truth slip.

PHASE IV
GENIUS LEADERSHIP

The idea of being a genius may make you uncomfortable but rest assured that you have aspects of genius in you. Everybody does. The humanized leader recognizes the genius in themselves and cultivates the genius in others.

As a leader, you may have a higher level of comfort observing and solving problems and seeing weakness areas for improvement. That requires the balance that comes from living in genius and purpose. That's the "strength" side of strengths and weaknesses.

This final phase of the Humanized Leader System asks you to dig deep to discover those activities that make your heart sing and fill you with strength and purpose. THAT is what will emanate to your team and clients, draw people to you, and create an environment where all are inspired to step up to all that they can be.

11

YOU ARE A GENIUS. IT'S TRUE!

Purpose

No book on leadership and leadership tools would be complete without a section on finding and creating your purpose. Leaders Inspired clients are taught to "lead on purpose," which reminds them of the intentionality of guiding, visioning for, mentoring, and leading others. Your leadership, then, must be rooted in something solid and grounding. Purpose does just that.

There are many teachers of purpose with many wonderful methods to access it. Many people start with a sorting of values until they are able to eliminate all but a few. Others look to the future and seek to understand what would be fulfilling to them and to humanity. Some use colors, emotions, or an examination of the lives of successful and values-based individuals.

Once you have sifted and sorted in whatever way is best for you, it is useful to create a statement of purpose, derived from your values, your experience with other leaders, and an acknowledgment of how and what you want to contribute to this time on earth.

When you have taken the time to identify these deeply rooted values that are a divining rod for decision-making and integrity-keeping, you will find a sturdiness in your leadership which will serve you well.

Purpose and Trees

Think of a tall and stately tree. The tree represents you as a leader. What makes the tree so sturdy and solid? It is, of course, the root system that digs deep into the earth, anchoring, nurturing, feeding, and stabilizing. The more established the tree, the deeper the root system. Your values are the root system that feeds the outward expression of your purpose (the tree).

A huge wind or brutal storm may come along and shake your tree like hell. You may lose some limbs and some leaves, yet at the end of the storm, you stand strong. Maybe you are a little battered, yet you are there. Your roots have anchored you.

This is how purpose works in your leadership. Temptation, clouded beliefs, wonky human behavior, tragedy, loss – all these things will inevitably present themselves. Welcome to the world of being human. Do you give up and chop down the tree? No…you allow the roots, your values, to stabilize you and make decisions that help the tree become healthy and vital again. Sometimes all that is needed is the passage of time.

What is Your Purpose?

I encourage you to find the way that is best for you to develop your values and purpose. Here is one method of creating your purpose statement.

Step One: Think about the contribution that you want to make in the world. If you were to leave this life today, what would you have offered to humanity? What are you creating, activating, or moving forward?

Step Two: What are you doing or who are you being while making your contribution? Would it be as a leader? Mother or father? Friend? Successful author? Are you teaching? Parenting? Listening? Offering feedback? Mentoring? Guiding? Verbs are best. Pick three of them.

Step Three: Think about a few leaders who have inspired you. These leaders could be personal to you or historical figures whom you admire. Find a quiet space, free from interruptions, and take about 20 minutes to reflect on these leaders. Why do they inspire you? What character traits made them a great leader? What did they cause you to do or think or achieve? What do you admire about them? Make a list of these characteristics. Consider them and choose up to three that you would like to be remembered for as you are doing what you do to make your contribution.

Step Four: Put it all together.

My purpose is to ____Contribution____, by ___being or doing__, ___being or doing__, being or doing___ with ___leader characteristic__, ___leader characteristic___, ___leader characteristic___.

Example from a Leadership Mastery student:

My purpose is to help people see what is possible for them, by teaching, listening, and coaching with compassion, courage, and never-ending optimism.

What does your purpose statement sound like?

Genius

You are a genius! How do you feel when you read that? Do you deflect? Do you demur? What?! Yes, you are a genius. We all are. You have something inside of you that drives you, motivates you, jazzes you. It's that thing that you can't wait to do, be, or have. You would do it every day for free if you had to.

Genius is an expression of your purpose that takes shape out in the world. It's the outward manifestation.

It's a tricky word, yes? Societally, you are taught to hide this part. It's ego. It's bragging. Granny will say, "your head is too big to get through the door." That's your comfort zone calling you back to the center of safety.

What if genius is your true comfort zone?

You need a balanced view of your leadership journey. Even though this book was written with encouragement and belief in you, you've largely focused on self-awareness and self-improvement up to this point. Time to look at the other side of the coin.

Your Challenge

Pull out a sheet of paper. Right now. Immediately. Follow these instructions and put the book to the side until you have completed the task.

- Set a timer for 10 minutes.
- Grab your pen.
- Write a list of 30 things that are great about you.

Some tips: write it all down, avoiding debate about whether it qualifies as great. If you get stuck, think of what a trusted friend would say, your dearest family member, your mentor, your best employee. Look at all aspects of yourself – mental, physical, spiritual, belongings, ways of thinking.

Go!

Done? Look in the mirror and read it out loud with intention. Better yet, find a trusted partner or colleague and read it aloud to them. You've got to own this!

This is a purposeful exercise that balances the scale of strengths and weaknesses. You must be able to know the wonderful and strong things about yourself as equally as you know that which needs improving. How can you do for others if you can't do it for yourself?

What Is Genius?

Dan Sullivan, founder and CEO of Strategic Coach, describes genius as "unique ability." Ask yourself, "What was I put here on Earth to do?"

Gaye Hendricks, author of *The Big Leap*, describes this as that one aspect that you "get" to do that brings you joy, energy, focus, expansion, creativity. The thing you leap out of bed each day to get started on, knowing the impact it will have on others and on oneself.

> "If you really want to fly, harness your power to your passion."
>
> – Oprah Winfrey

Genius is innate ability coming face to face with creativity, energy, and passion. What are you passionate about? Where has that shown up in your life? Where has your passion become a high-level of competence?

When you know this, assess where you are spending most of your time. If it's not where your genius can shine, find a way to get there more often. You will be amazed at what you are able to create in less time and with less effort.

Everyone has an ego. Ego, made famous by Sigmund Freud, is defined as the opinion that you have about yourself, a part of the mind that senses and adapts to the real world.

The ego has a useful function. It helps to discern, to understand, and to set boundaries, as well as to remember, evaluate, and plan.

Spiritual and personal development decry the ego, insisting that the ego must be subdued or diminished or obliterated. Key transformational leaders will avow that they have transcended their ego.

Bad news. You still have one. As an emotionally intelligent leader, you want to spend more time in genius and therefore you must learn to manage the ego in the same way that you manage emotions:

1. Recognize and don't deny.
2. Clean up any ego explosions.
3. Find neutrality – that purposeful and passionate place of presence in your mind and spirit that resists ego and emotional hooks or triggers.

When ego is denied or justified, leading one into drama rather than purpose, you are not aligned with emotional intelligence.

One of the tricky things about the ego is that it enjoys safety and protection, both of "yourself" and "itself." When ego is running the show, you often find yourself in resistance and protection, becoming masked and defensive. Boy, that commitment to safety takes a lot of energy.

Consider the acronym: EGO is **E**asing **G**enius **O**ut. Ego contains push and pull, contrast and comparison, levels and closed doors.

Genius is flow. Genius is open, honoring, emotionally vibrant, and unconcerned with the safety and protection of its neighbor, EGO.

When leading an emotionally intelligent life, you will find yourself in the flow of genius more and more often and ego subterfuge will become easier to see. You have choices:

- Flow or resist
- Create or compare
- Curious or critical

The first choice is easier. Learn to dance between healthy expressions of ego and living in your genius.

Recognizing the Genius in Others - Delegation

Sometimes it's easier to see the genius in others. As we plan our work product, we may notice that a team member has raw talent in some domain or an extra drive to deliver.

Your job as a leader is to identify these qualities and cultivate them. Delegate what is not found in your own genius activities (that you are still working on and improving!) to another person who will get to play in their genius.

You can download a formula, checklist and chart to help you delegate with greater strength here: www.thehumanizedleader.com/bonus

In Summary: the Genius Zone

- When purpose and genius collide, there you find your passionate, unique ability
- You have a choice to spend your time in competency or genius
- Genius is ego-free, joyful, and energy boosting
- A key skill to find 20% more time in your genius is to notice the genius in others
- When you notice the genius in others, delegate liberally

Appreciation

Appreciation is a key tool in the leadership toolkit if you want to create fabulous results, highly motivated teams, and a lot of joy and expansion in the work that you do.

> "There is more hunger for love and appreciation in this world than for bread."
> — Mother Teresa

There is a difference between praise and appreciation. Praise, often expressed as "atta boy," "you're so smart," or other vague platitudes, does not speak to value, worth, or impact. It's perceived as insincere. You, as a leader, may view praise as a box to check, a task to complete. But appreciation goes much further than praise. Appreciation is an active expression of gratitude, sincerely acknowledging the other's character or beingness, or the impact they have on you personally or the business globally. It is specific and customized to that person.

As an emotionally intelligent leader, you must be facile at offering sincere and specific appreciation often and role model grace in receiving it. Many people have difficulty in the receiving category.

People are Masters at Deflecting and Withholding Appreciation

The Deflection. You receive a compliment (a kissing cousin to praise) about the outfit you are wearing. You reply, "Oh, this, this old dress, I've had it for 10 years!" thereby deflecting the compliment.

The Turnaround. Uncomfortable when someone sincerely brings attention to your work effort with appreciation, you immediately take the spotlight from yourself and turn the conversation to the other person.

The Withhold. You fail to offer appreciation to other people even when it is warranted. An oddly misplaced perception of power enables a false belief that if you appreciate somebody it gives them power over you. Or do you fear the other will now expect something from you? Do you hold the belief that appreciation is not needed, that your team members are just doing what you pay them for?

The Fear. You may have a fear of appearing insincere. Perhaps you fear that you will look silly or sound awkward or that your appreciation will be rejected in some way.

The Oblivion. You don't pay attention and appreciation does not become conscious or intentional. You are paying attention to the finish line, the problems, results to be achieved. You go go go go, forgetting that along each mile marker of achievement are other people who are supporting the effort. Stop for a moment, smell the roses, and offer appreciation. Sometimes we're moving too fast to do so.

A Realer Reason. At the root of it, you likely avoid appreciation because it causes you to feel vulnerable. *Appreciation creates vulnerability – on both sides*. It makes you vulnerable. Vulnerability is uncomfortable and the comfort zone is welcoming you back again.

Remember, EQ Leader, there is strength in your vulnerability. Being vulnerable enables your true humility, makes you approachable, creates connection, and builds trust. So does appreciation.

Be the Change You Wish to See in the World. Offer Appreciation.

As a business leader you may be asking yourself the question: "What do I need to do to truly express appreciation?" Here are some things to remember:

- Be genuine and say only what you really mean.
- Be specific about describing your experience and use details to do so.

- Describe how others have positively impacted you or the business.
- Let others know the benefit that you have received from this.
- Use words that convey emotion.

How do you feel about it?

Be purposeful, restating the appreciation using different words or ideas to help the person get it. Make sure that the communication hits the target.

Be the Change You Wish to See in the World. Receive Appreciation.

Sometimes it's not easy to receive appreciation especially if we lack confidence or self-esteem. Here's what you need to remember when someone is offering you a compliment or their sincere appreciation:

- Stand strong in the conversation, avoiding any false humility that urges you to deflect.
- Hear the words and the underlying emotion.
- Accept it.
- Say "thank you" without debate or justification.

Simply by saying "Thank you " you are taking a step towards an acceptance of your inner genius. There is no need for quid pro quo here. Simply receive.

Sawubona

The Zulu people of southern Africa have a beautiful greeting that conveys appreciation for one another. As other cultures might say, "How are you?" the Zulu says, "Sawubona." Their beautiful greeting, "Sawubona," extends appreciation and is well placed in this talk of EQ Leadership.

Simply translated, Sawubona means "I value you; I respect you; I see you and you are important to me." That is an incredible articulation of deep appreciation for others.

A sincere expression of appreciation is needed now more than ever. Our fast-paced, results-driven, technologically-motivated workforces can become dehumanizing. Appreciation restores the human connection. People need other people. Connected people who feel appreciated and involved create good outcomes. *Sawubona.* The world needs your appreciation right now. We've got some work to do on this planet and it won't happen quite so easily without appreciation.

Personal Perspective

From my heart to yours. My mom passed away several years ago after a lingering illness. Although sad to lose a loved one, I felt complete in my appreciation for her. I had plenty of time to express it to her and honor the impact she had on my life.

We had time.

The very same day, a young man who was a friend of my children passed away. He was at the very start of his life, in his early twenties. His family and his friends had no idea. They had no precognition that anything would be happening to impact the life of this young man when he passed away.

I looked at the outpouring of appreciation that overflowed on his social media. I'm still touched today remembering the hundreds of people who were motivated to go to his Facebook page and express their appreciation of how this young man had touched their lives. The words were almost too much to bear in their sincerity and specificity.

I wondered if he was aware of the impact that he had had on all these people while he was living. Did he realize the specific ways he had made a difference? Maybe at some level he did, and maybe few bothered to express their appreciation to him while he was alive.

I committed from that day that I would be copious in my specific and sincere appreciation. I would look for the opportunities to acknowledge and express the impact that others have had and continue to have on me. I want to make sure that people hear it, feel it, and integrate it while living their lives. I want it to propel people forward in confidence and self-awareness. I want to appreciate it while living. I don't want to wait to post it on a Facebook page when life has ended.

Sawubona.

Find a way each day to let somebody who is important to you know that they are valued, that they're respected, and that they're important to you.

The 17th century poet John Milton says gratitude (appreciation) bestows reverence, changing forever how we experience life and the world. You will never know what your expression of appreciation might do for another human being today and so I want to support you to create an environment of appreciation.

Put It Into Practice

Here are ten actions you can take to build up your appreciation muscle. Take some notes, pay attention, put something into action, and see what joy and magic you can create in your life.

- Make it personal. Start by appreciating yourself. What do you appreciate about you?
- Keep a gratitude journal.
- Send appreciation cards. Write out your appreciation and send the physical card to another person.
- Count your blessings and then recount them to the person who helped you to create them.
- Practice forgiveness. Everybody benefits from a bit of slack, yourself and others included.
- Acknowledge the little details. What's that little extra that you can offer, what's that little extra that you are noticing? It doesn't have to be grand and swooping. It could be one small contribution to an outcome that you appreciate.
- Make a choice. You are in charge of your feelings, your thoughts, and your actions. You are the creator of your own life, so choose gratitude and appreciation.
- Get into the habit of noticing things for which you are grateful. They are all around you. Make noticing and expressing your appreciation a daily practice.
- Make a game out of it. Create check marks.

- Write it in your journal to memorialize your appreciation. What you pay attention to expands.
- And finally, don't delay. You may think you have all the time in the world, but you don't. Let the people you care about know how much you appreciate them today.

In Closing

You are deeply appreciated for taking leadership so seriously and for committing to increasing your emotional intelligence. You are deeply appreciated for taking specific actions with your teams and families. You are appreciated for the relentless self-inquiry that is a part of this journey.

It is a privilege to witness your leadership journey.

Regular expressions of appreciation become a way of being. See it as part of your leadership integrity.

And don't forget about karma. Although you offer your appreciation expecting nothing in return, you must know by now that what you give will always come back to you in abundance.

The famous transformational author, Wayne Dyer, has said, "Give yourself the gift of five minutes of contemplation in awe of everything that you see around you." Go outside and bring your attention to the many miracles around you.

Spend the day in appreciation and see what magic you can create.

Action Steps

1. Consider your genius by completing the following:
   1. Make a list of those things you are doing where you have mediocre results or very little interest.
   2. What of this can you delegate and to whom?
2. Make a list of those things you are doing where you are competent but other people could easily do them as good or better than you.
   1. What of this can you delegate and to whom?

3. Make a list of those things where you are excellent and regularly get affirmation and acknowledgement of good performance from others.
    1. Who on your team are you willing to develop to the level of excellence you currently enjoy?
4. Now...make a list of all the work or life activities and experiences that bring you joy, feel effortless, bring meaning to you and to where you are inherently drawn.
    1. Make a plan to spend 20% more of your time in these activities.
    2. Express appreciation in some form each and every day.

12

YOUR LEADERSHIP HEART BEATS WITH STRENGTH

Good for you. You made it to the end. You must be kidding, right? The end? This is only the beginning.

Here's what you now must do:

Throw it all away.

Every tool, every trick, every tidbit, every piece of advice – throw it ALL away. You've learned it and it is inside of you as a hidden roadmap. You don't need to pull it out and look at it and study it anymore.

Now, the hard work – the brilliant, tender, tough, challenging, and most rewarding work of all – begins. That is the work of connecting with the people around you in a way that makes them feel valuable, listened to, important, invested, and alive. Because of your leadership.

There are no tricks or tips to this; there is only heartfelt connection and a good conversation.

Have the conversations that make you feel jittery, that scare you. Have them from the heart, knowing you have already incorporated any leadership "muscle memory" from the work you have undertaken with this book.

From the Client Vault

Let me tell you the story of John. John was the general manager of a prime property in a major hotel chain. The GM is a big deal – part parent, part general, part cheerleader – to those who work under their guidance. John's property was a "select service" hotel which provides a hearty breakfast to lodgers. Most properties of this sort have a special breakfast server, an older woman who is much like a beloved aunt or grandmother, who oversees caring for the guests during breakfast service.

John's property had Betsy. Betsy showed up to love her guests five days out of the week. And she had love to offer, for sure. One person she loved was John. One thing she loved most was talking to John – and talking and talking and talking.

One day, John casually mentioned that he was taking his family to Wisconsin. Guess where Miss Betsy was from? You got it. From that day forward, it became her loving mission in life to talk to John about Wisconsin each and every day. Stories were told, and repeated, and expanded – all regaling Wisconsin.

As you can imagine, this soon wore on John. The conversations happened every morning and lasted ten or more minutes. He tried sneaking in a side door. She found him. He tried coming in before her. She still snagged him. He tried being rude to her. It rolled off her back like water on a Wisconsin duck.

He walked into his Leadership Mastery group one day and announced that he simply was going to have to fire Miss Betsy. She was driving him crazy and could not effectively run his business with her around. John's position was not affirmed by the rest of the group. The entire class called him to a higher standard and put him on notice that he had not fully stepped into his leadership role. He hadn't had the kinds of lovingly direct conversations with Miss Betsy to correct what was judged to be misspent time.

We advised him to scroll through the tools he had learned:

1. He had stepped too fully into the concepts of modern leadership which can sometimes blur boundaries and felt that he had to give Miss Betsy his full attention every time he was approached.
2. He was avoiding conflict and failing to apply direct, factual, neutral, and kind direction.

3.   He forgot the fundamental principle of EQ: that other people have emotions and desires and the job of the leader is to invest in the relationship.
4.   He was squarely in victimhood and on his way to villainy.
5.   He was listening from the point of view of his own agenda of finishing it off swiftly (which is non-listening).
6.   He did not provide appropriate feedback.
7.   There was no encouragement.
8.   He was not able to see, let alone own, his contribution to the situation.
9.   Genius and unique ability were thrown out the window.
10.   He not only did not appreciate her, he began to resent her.

In his frustration, the tools didn't matter because he wasn't using them anyway.

His peers encouraged him to use the tools he had learned. He needed to both honor the emotional need of Miss Betsy and reclaim ten to thirty minutes of his precious time each day. He had to have a loving, boundary-setting conversation. There was nobody in the class of his peers who would stand by his position of needing to fire her.

He decided to change his reaction to a response and had a loving, human conversation with Miss Betsy where he set a visit limit of a few minutes each day. During those two minutes or so, he could fully and completely devote his time, energy, and attention to whatever was important for her to talk about. At the end of the two minutes, he invited her back into their mutual purpose of caring for and loving the guests.

This continued until the day she retired. His resentment was gone, Miss Betsy was honored, and the guests were still cared for.

Fast forward several years later when John was informed of Miss Betsy's passing. He respectfully attended her services. During the visitation, he was approached by an elderly lady who looked a lot like Miss Betsy.

"Are you Mr. John?"

"Yes, I am."

"I'm Mary, Betsy's sister. Thank you, John. You have no idea the pleasure that you brought to Betsy's life. There wasn't a day that she came home from the hotel where she didn't talk about the conversations she had with you. You made her very happy. Thank you."

This is based upon a true story. You never know what ripple you are creating in another person's life when you keep the right leadership tools in your hip pocket, forget about them until you really need them, and use them with confidence. When you tell another what you need in a loving way and have the difficult heart-to-heart conversations when they're needed, you build trust and deeper relationships. You create impact!

Take responsibility for the quality of your connections from a clear and loving heart. You will always be led in a good direction. If you need a tune-up, pull out a tool. But never, ever, ever, rely on a tool instead of a conversation.

Remember your humanity. Remember that it is a privilege to lead. Remember that you are the Humanized Leader.

You've got this!

Over and out.

CONCLUDING THOUGHTS

Thank you for taking this journey with me. It was my privilege to be your guide. I believe so strongly in your Humanized Leadership and its ability to inspire and uplift.

Take a moment to join our community at www.thehumanized-leader.com.

The more of us who are heartfelt, secure, solid, and HUMAN in our leadership, the more likely we will be able to shift the world to kindness, satisfaction, and joy.

REVIEW INQUIRY

Hey, it's Mary Pat Knight here.

I hope you've enjoyed the book, finding it both useful and fun. I have a favor to ask you.

Would you consider giving it a rating wherever you bought the book? Online book stores are more likely to promote a book when they feel good about its content, and reader reviews are a great barometer for a book's quality.

So please go to the website of wherever you bought the book, search for my name and the book title, and leave a review. If able, perhaps consider adding a picture of you holding the book. That increases the likelihood your review will be accepted!

Many thanks in advance,

Mary Pat Knight

WILL YOU SHARE THE LOVE?

Get this book for a friend, associate or family member!

If you have found this book valuable and know others who would find it useful, consider buying them a copy as a gift. Special bulk discounts are available if you would like your whole team or organization to benefit from reading this. Just contact support@leadersinspired.com or visit the webpage at www.thehumanizedleader.com.

WOULD YOU LIKE MARY PAT KNIGHT TO SPEAK TO YOUR ORGANIZATION?

Book Mary Pat Now!

Mary Pat accepts a limited number of speaking, coaching, and corporate training engagements each year. To learn how you can bring her message to your organization, email support@leadersinspired.com.

ABOUT THE AUTHOR

Mary Pat Knight

Mary Pat Knight is a speaker, author, coach, and consultant who is an expert in leadership and emotional intelligence. Her 30-year career spans executive leadership positions in marketing, operations, strategic planning, human resources, management and employee development, and executive coaching.

She is the Visionary for Leaders Inspired, a global training and development firm dedicated to personal and team leadership transformation.

The Humanized Leader is based upon her simple, yet powerful system for creating Emotional Intelligence, robust leadership ,and transformative cultures. She has helped thousands to express themselves authentically, work from a place of courage, and find an inner unshakeable belief in themselves. She teaches others how to lead both personally and professionally in integrity and free of compromise.

Her mission is to inspire business transformation and develop solid leadership, remembering that when you are inspired in the workplace, you inspire the world.

Mary Pat can be reached at: support@leadersinspired.com, www.leadersinspired.com and www.thehumanizedleader.com

www.ingramcontent.com/pod-product-compliance
Lightning Source LLC
Chambersburg PA
CBHW071416210326
41597CB00020B/3530